For exams in 2023

ICAEW
Business Planning: Taxation

TP06-7-30523-0002

First edition 2013, Eleventh edition 2022

ISBN 978-1-0355-0197-7

British Library Cataloguing-in-Publication Data

A catalogue record for this book is available from the British Library

Published by

BPP Learning Media Ltd
BPP House, Aldine Place
142–144 Uxbridge Road
London W12 8AA

www.bpp.com/learningmedia

Printed in the United Kingdom

Welcome to BPP Learning Media's **Passcards** for ICAEW **Business Planning: Taxation.**

- They **save you time**. Important topics are summarised for you.

- They incorporate **diagrams** to kick start your memory.

- They follow the overall **structure** of the ICAEW Workbook, but BPP Learning Media's ICAEW **Passcards** are not just a condensed book. Each card has been separately designed for clear presentation. Topics are self contained and can be grasped visually.

- ICAEW **Passcards** are **just the right size** for pockets, briefcases and bags.

- ICAEW **Passcards focus on the exams** you will be facing.

Run through the **Passcards** as often as you can during your final revision period. The day before the exam, try to go through the **Passcards** again! You will then be well on your way to passing your exams.

Good luck!

Contents

1: Ethics

Your advice in relation to transactions must comply with the law and the ICAEW Code of Ethics.

You must apply scepticism and ethical judgement to a given scenario to determine the true facts and make reasoned suggestions for actions to take in relation to a given ethical dilemma.

You must be able to apply the ICAEW Code of Ethics, the Professional Conduct in Relation to Taxation, and/or anti-money laundering rules to a scenario to reach a reasoned solution.

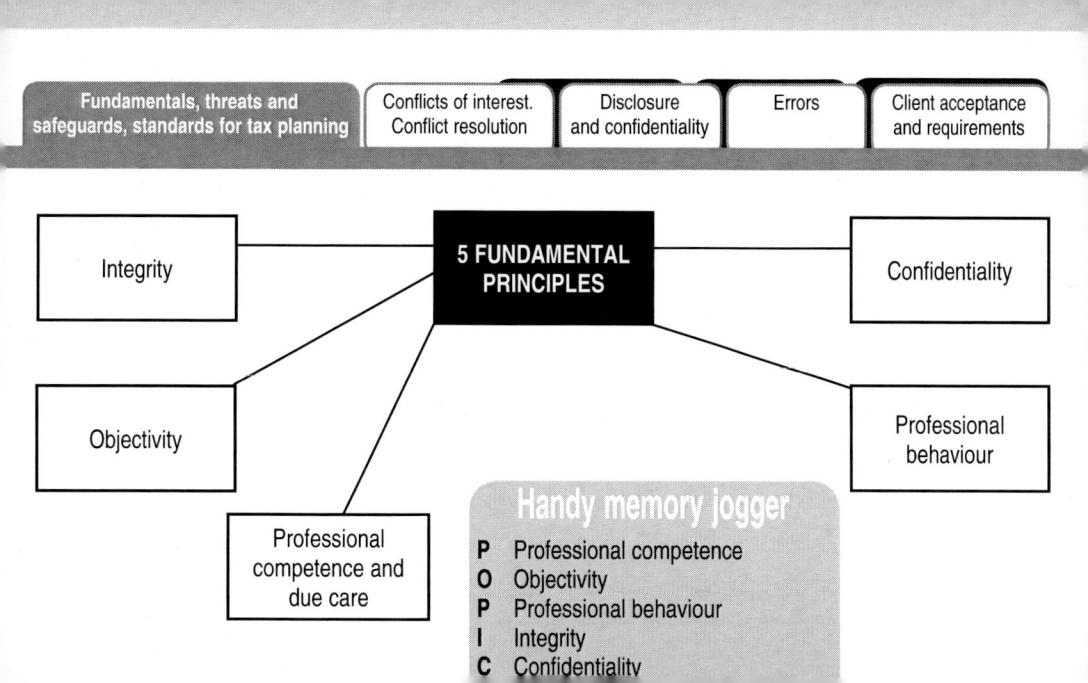

Integrity

Objectivity

5 FUNDAMENTAL PRINCIPLES

Confidentiality

Professional behaviour

Professional competence and due care

Handy memory jogger

P   Professional competence
O   Objectivity
P   Professional behaviour
I   Integrity
C   Confidentiality

Threats and safeguards framework

Threats to compliance
- Self-interest threats
- Self-review threats
- Advocacy threats
- Familiarity threats
- Intimidation threats

Safeguards
- Educational, training and experience
- CPD
- Corporate governance
- Professional standards
- Monitoring and disciplinary procedures
- External review

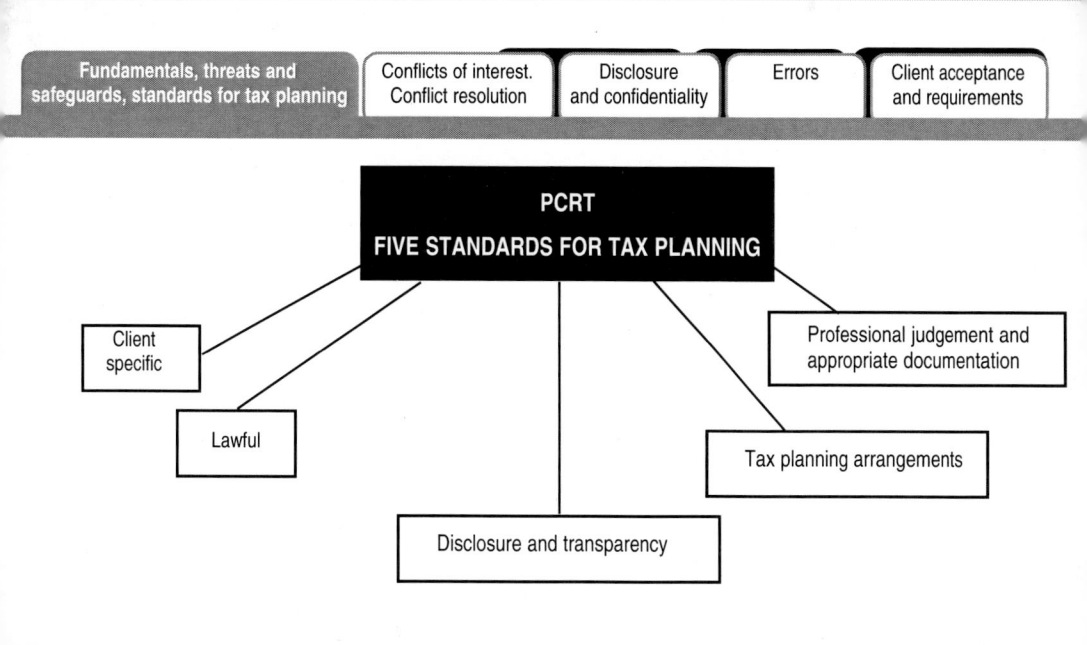

> Should take reasonable steps to identify circumstances that could pose a conflict of interest.

Conflict situations

Where a firm acts for both:

- Financial involvements between client and firm (eg, loan)
- Spouses in a divorce settlement
- A company and its directors in their personal capacity
- Partnership and partners in their personal capacity
- Two competing businesses

Consider:
- Separate engagement teams
- Clear guidelines for teams
- Confidentiality agreements
- Regular reviews

Alert! Do not act if one of the five fundamental principles is unacceptably threatened.

Safeguards

- Notify the client of the conflict of interest
- Notify all parties that acting for two or more parties in a conflict matter
- Notify the client that not acting exclusively for any one client
- Obtain consent of the relevant parties to act

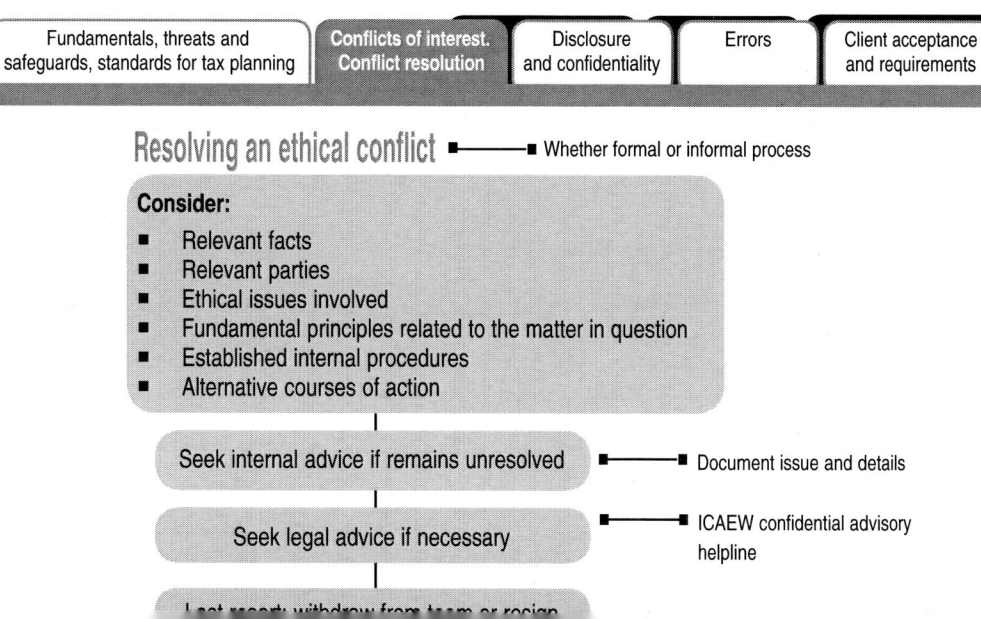

Resolving an ethical conflict ■━━━■ Whether formal or informal process

Consider:

- Relevant facts
- Relevant parties
- Ethical issues involved
- Fundamental principles related to the matter in question
- Established internal procedures
- Alternative courses of action

Seek internal advice if remains unresolved ■━━━■ Document issue and details

Seek legal advice if necessary ■━━━■ ICAEW confidential advisory helpline

Last resort: withdraw from team or resign

Allowed to disclose confidential information:

1 When **authorised** by the client or employer

2 When **required by law** to do so:

- Production of documents for legal proceedings

- Disclosure to the appropriate public authorities eg, under anti-money laundering legislation

3 When there is a **professional duty** or right to do so

Consider

- Will disclosure harm any interested party's interests?
- Is all known information correct?
- Is type of communication and recipient appropriate?
- Is information privileged?
- What are the legal and regulatory obligations and the possible implications of disclosure?
- Whether all facts have been confirmed and recorded

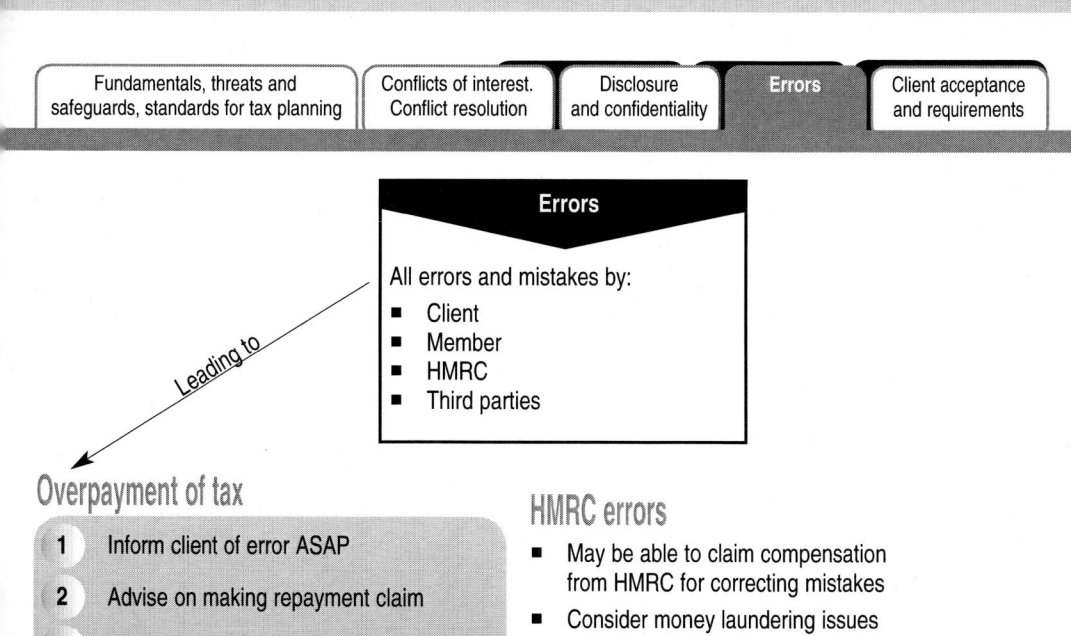

Errors

All errors and mistakes by:

- Client
- Member
- HMRC
- Third parties

Leading to

Overpayment of tax

1. Inform client of error ASAP

2. Advise on making repayment claim

3. Consider time limits

HMRC errors

- May be able to claim compensation from HMRC for correcting mistakes

- Consider money laundering issues

- May need to notif. PII insurers ▶▶ See below

Engagement letter

Contractual relationship – detailing responsibilities of:

- Client
- Professional accountant

Authority to disclose for inclusion in the engagement letter:

- HMRC error
- Disclosure required by law
- Professional right or duty to disclose

Responsibility for tax returns

Client responsible for accuracy and completeness of the return

Accountant to obtain client's written approval of the return

Accountant may submit the return on behalf of the client in certain circumstances

May advise fuller disclosure if significant tax planning or doubt

Professional indemnity insurance

- Required if ICAEW qualified member in public practice

- Minimum requirement:

    - Gross fee income < £600,000

        - 2½ times gross fee income
        - Minimum £100,000

    - Otherwise minimum = £1.5 million

- Cover

    - Must remain in place for at least two years after ceases public practice

    - Six years is recommended

Data protection

- Notify Information Commissioner's Office (ICO) who monitors compliance with GDPR

- Criminal offence if fail to notify

If company has:

- Turnover > £200 million and/or
- Balance sheet > £2 billion

Duties of SAOs
senior accounting officer

- SAO must certify annually that accounting systems are adequate for accurate tax reporting

- Failure – criminal offence

Anti-money laundering and counter-terrorist financing

Attempt to conceal the true origin or ownership of the proceeds of criminal activity or terrorist funding ('criminal property')

Must register with an appropriate anti-money laundering supervisory authority.

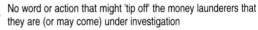

1 Client checking, record keeping and internal suspicion reporting

Appointment of a Money Laundering Reporting Officer (MLRO); client checking procedures

2 Not doing or discussing anything that might prejudice an investigation

No word or action that might 'tip off' the money launderers that they are (or may come) under investigation

3 Report suspicions (on reasonable grounds) of money laundering/terrorist financing ⌐

Report to:

- The Money Laundering Reporting Officer
- National Crime Agency (use suspicious activity report (SAR))

└ Watch client confidentiality

Penalties: Offences tried in Magistrates' Court or Crown Court – unlimited fines and imprisonment possible

AML levy: From 2023/24 for firms in the AML regulated sector of a fixed amount determined by the size of the firm.

Tax avoidance

- Legal tax effective method of avoiding/reducing amount of tax due
- No intention of misleading HMRC

Acceptable tax avoidance – using available reliefs

Aggressive tax avoidance – may be questioned by HMRC

Signposts:

- Disproportionate tax benefits
- Artificiality
- Circular transactions

Tax planning

- Minimising tax liability using tax incentives
- Eg, individuals using ISAs
- Eg, companies using R&D relief

Data analytics help to reduce the tax gap (difference between tax owed and tax received).

From April 2022, businesses taking uncertain tax positions in their tax returns will be required to notify HMRC of this.

Tax evasion

- Illegal way of avoiding/reducing amount of tax due
- Misleading HMRC eg,

    1 Suppressing information

    2 Providing deliberately false information

- Accountants (partnerships/companies) may commit an offence if they fail to prevent facilitation of tax evasion (Criminal Finances Act 2017).

Company directors may be jointly and severally liable with the company for a tax liability if there is a risk of insolvency and:

| Tax avoidance | and BEPS | avoidance schemes |

General anti-abuse rule (GAAR)

HMRC can counteract arrangements if:
- Obtaining tax advantage was one of their main purposes
- They are abusive

Can also use **Ramsay doctrine** to attack tax avoidance

60% penalty

Make just and reasonable adjustments

Refer to Independent Advisory Panel

If:
- entering into them; or
- carrying them out

is not a reasonable course of action

Important case law

Ramsay Ltd v IRC and other cases
- Disregard transactions with no commercial purpose
- But not always eg, where purpose of legislation unclear
- Success of aggressive tax avoidance is uncertain

Base erosion and profit shifting (BEPS)

Actions to tackle companies' attempts to artificially reduce income eg:
- CFC provisions
- Transfer pricing rules
- Diverted profits tax ⟫ see Ch 15
- Patent box regime ⟫ see Ch 9

BEPS 2.0 particularly seeks to address the taxation of e-commerce income.

1: Ethics

DOTAS & DASVOIT schemes

Notify HMRC where:

- Person obtains/might obtain tax advantage
- Main/one of the main benefits of the arrangement
- Notify HMRC if scheme falls within at least one **hallmark**
- May have to pay tax up-front (accelerated payment)

Hallmarks

- Confidentiality
- Premium fee
- Standardised tax products
- Others specific to DOTAS
- Others specific to DASVOIT

- Promoter must notify HMRC within five days of making scheme available and for DASVOIT within 30 days of VAT being different due to the scheme
- Register with HMRC
- Penalties for failure to comply:
  - Disclosure penalty
  - Information penalty

Promoter = responsible for design, management, marketing etc

Unless has reasonable excuse

May receive a conduct notice if triggers a threshold condition

Alert! Information provided to HMRC regarding breach of DOTAS or DASVOIT rules does not breach

Failure to report scheme

2: Income tax and NIC

Topic List

Revision from Tax Compliance

Individual Savings Accounts (ISAs)

Venture capital

This chapter reviews certain NIC and income tax topics covered in the Tax Compliance exam.

It then deals with Individual Savings Accounts (ISAs) which allow all taxpayers, whatever their risk profile, to invest in tax free investments.

We then cover the rules for the various venture capital schemes, which aim to attract investors who are not averse to taking risks with their investments in return for valuable tax breaks.

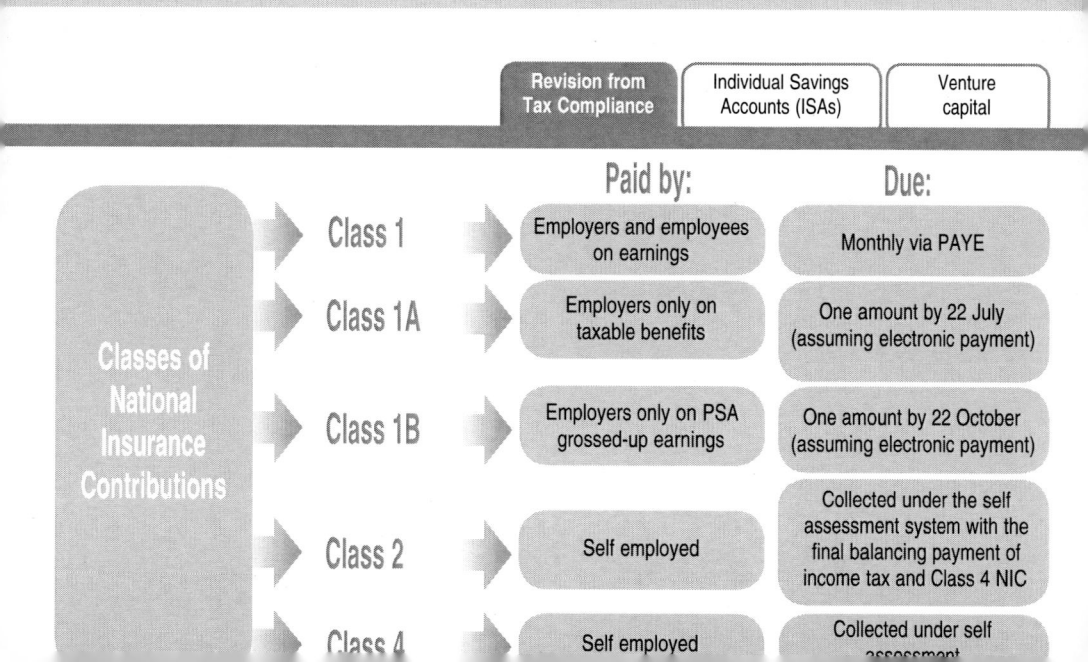

Classes of National Insurance Contributions

	Paid by:	Due:
Class 1	Employers and employees on earnings	Monthly via PAYE
Class 1A	Employers only on taxable benefits	One amount by 22 July (assuming electronic payment)
Class 1B	Employers only on PSA grossed-up earnings	One amount by 22 October (assuming electronic payment)
Class 2	Self employed	Collected under the self assessment system with the final balancing payment of income tax and Class 4 NIC
Class 4	Self employed	Collected under self assessment

Health and social care levy

1.25% on earnings subject to NIC (and earnings for workers over pensionable age) from 2023/24. For 2022/23 NIC rates have been temporarily increased by 1.25%.

CLASS 1

Primary

Employees pay contributions of 13.25% of **earnings** between the primary earnings threshold and the upper earnings limit; 3.25% on earnings above the upper earnings limit.

- Includes payments over the statutory mileage rate. Always use 45ppm

- Paid for an earnings period eg, weekly, monthly (annual if director)

- Paid from age 16 to pensionable age

Secondary

Employers pay contributions of 15.05% on all earnings above the secondary earnings threshold.

- Reduced by £5,000 employment allowance if prior year liability less than £100k

- Paid for:
  - Employees 21+
  - Apprentices 25+
- Only payable for employees < 21 and apprentices < 25 on earnings > upper secondary threshold

CLASS 1A

Employers pay Class 1A contributions at 15.05% on most **taxable benefits** provided to their employees.

CLASS 1B

Payable by employers at 15.05% on the grossed-up value of earnings included in a **PAYE settlement agreement (PSA)**.

The self employed (ie, sole traders and partners) pay Class 2 **and** Class 4 NICs.

Class 2

Class 2 NIC is calculated at a flat weekly rate.

■ No contributions are payable if the individual's profits are below the small profits threshold and at 0% if below the lower profits limit.

Class 4

Class 4 NICs are 10.25% of any **profits** falling between an upper and lower profits limit and 3.25% above upper profits limit.

■ Profits are the tax adjusted profits

■ Can reduce by available trading losses (even where set against non-trading income in previous years)

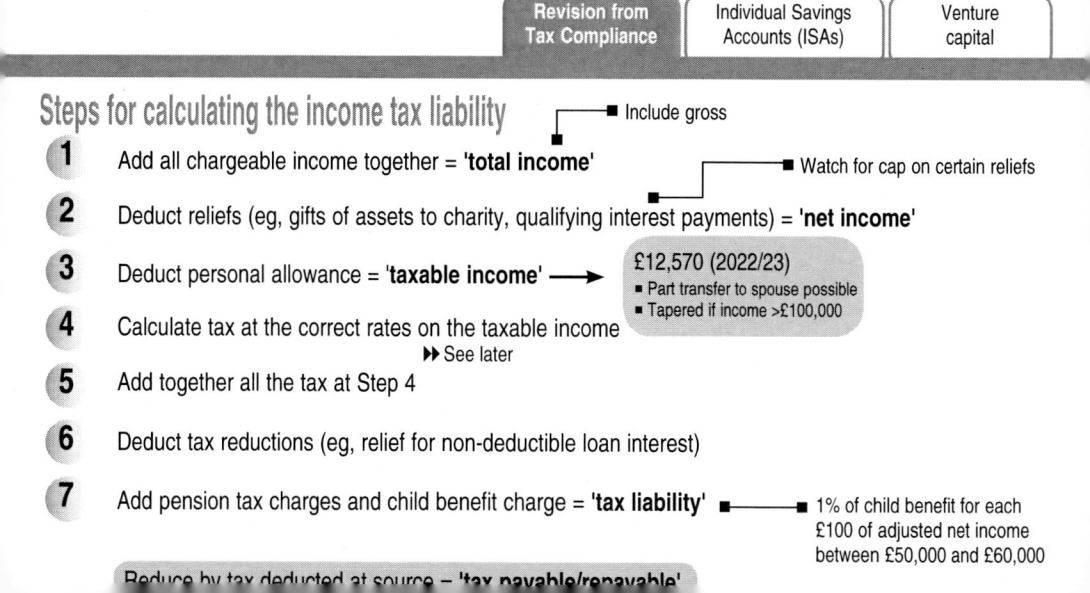

Steps for calculating the income tax liability

■ Include gross

1 Add all chargeable income together = **'total income'**

■ Watch for cap on certain reliefs

2 Deduct reliefs (eg, gifts of assets to charity, qualifying interest payments) = **'net income'**

3 Deduct personal allowance = **'taxable income'** →

£12,570 (2022/23)
■ Part transfer to spouse possible
■ Tapered if income >£100,000

4 Calculate tax at the correct rates on the taxable income
▶▶ See later

5 Add together all the tax at Step 4

6 Deduct tax reductions (eg, relief for non-deductible loan interest)

7 Add pension tax charges and child benefit charge = **'tax liability'** ■

■ 1% of child benefit for each £100 of adjusted net income between £50,000 and £60,000

Reduce by tax deducted at source = **'tax payable/repayable'**

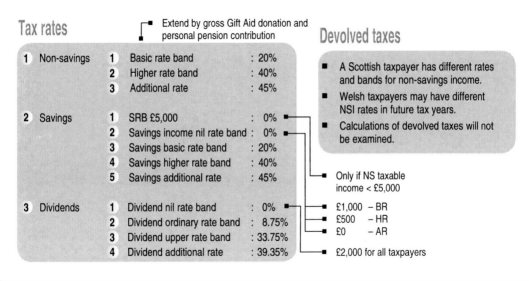

Tax rates

Extend by gross Gift Aid donation and personal pension contribution

1	Non-savings	1	Basic rate band	: 20%
		2	Higher rate band	: 40%
		3	Additional rate	: 45%

2	Savings	1	SRB £5,000	: 0%
		2	Savings income nil rate band	: 0%
		3	Savings basic rate band	: 20%
		4	Savings higher rate band	: 40%
		5	Savings additional rate	: 45%

3	Dividends	1	Dividend nil rate band	: 0%
		2	Dividend ordinary rate band	: 8.75%
		3	Dividend upper rate band	: 33.75%
		4	Dividend additional rate	: 39.35%

Devolved taxes

- A Scottish taxpayer has different rates and bands for non-savings income.
- Welsh taxpayers may have different NSI rates in future tax years.
- Calculations of devolved taxes will not be examined.

- Only if NS taxable income < £5,000
- £1,000 – BR
- £500 – HR
- £0 – AR
- £2,000 for all taxpayers

Exempt income

- Interest on NS&I certificates
- Income arising on ISAs
- Betting and lottery winnings
- Premium bond winnings
- Certain social security benefits
- First £7,500 of rent under rent a room scheme
- Scholarships
- Income tax repayment interest
- Dividends on shares in a VCT
- Payments under Compensation schemes eg, Windrush Compensation Scheme
- Apprenticeship bursary paid to care leavers

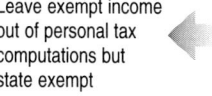

Leave exempt income out of personal tax computations but state exempt

Apprenticeship levy

- For employers with pay bill > £3 million
- 0.5% annual pay bill
- Payable monthly

ISA accounts

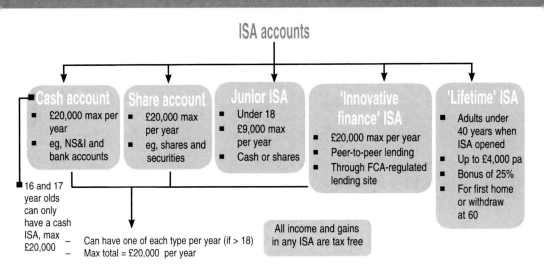

Cash account
- £20,000 max per year
- eg, NS&I and bank accounts

Share account
- £20,000 max per year
- eg, shares and securities

Junior ISA
- Under 18
- £9,000 max per year
- Cash or shares

'Innovative finance' ISA
- £20,000 max per year
- Peer-to-peer lending
- Through FCA-regulated lending site

'Lifetime' ISA
- Adults under 40 years when ISA opened
- Up to £4,000 pa
- Bonus of 25%
- For first home or withdraw at 60

■ 16 and 17 year olds can only have a cash ISA, max £20,000

- Can have one of each type per year (if > 18)
- Max total = £20,000 per year

All income and gains in any ISA are tax free

Enterprise Investment Scheme (EIS)

Investments subscribed for in the ordinary shares of unlisted trading companies, carrying on a qualifying trade, provide a tax reduction, saving income tax of 30% × investment

If the shares are not retained for at least three years the tax reduction is wholly or partly withdrawn

Max investment = £1 million a year or £2 million if investing in KICs

Reduction given in the tax year of investment or previous year

Knowledge Intensive Companies

Note: Gains made more than three years after the share issue are usually exempt from CGT

Qualifying company

- Carry on qualifying trade (no financial, asset-backed or renewable energy generation trades)
- Permanent establishment in the UK
- Unquoted
- Assets ≤ £15m before and ≤ £16m after issue
- < 250 full-time equivalent employees (< 500 for knowledge-intensive companies)
- ≤ £5m raised in previous 12 months, or £10m for KICs
- < £12m raised in total under EIS/VCT schemes (< £20m if knowledge-intensive company)
- Raised monies within 7 yrs of 1st commercial sale (10 yrs if knowledge-intensive)
- Not in financial difficulty

Investor

Must not be connected with the company ie, must not:
- Be an employee (or non-qualifying director); or
- Own > 30% of ordinary shares/voting rights; or
- Hold other shares in the company ── Unless founder shares or from a risk finance investment

EIS deferral relief

A gain realised by an individual on any asset can be deferred when the individual subscribes for new (ordinary shares) in an EIS company in the period commencing one year before and ending three years after the disposal.

The investor can be connected with the EIS company (eg, own >30% of the shares)

Business asset disposal relief available if would have been available for original disposal

- The shares do not need to attract EIS income tax relief.
- A qualifying company is an unquoted company carrying on a qualifying trade.
- The gain is 'frozen' and becomes chargeable if the shares are sold at any time or if certain events happen (eg, taxpayer ceases to be UK resident within the three years following issue of shares).
- A **claim** may be for any specified amount of the gain, up to the cost of the shares.

Can make use of available capital losses and annual exempt amount

Disposal of EIS shares

Gain

Exempt if disposal
> 3 years after
subscription

Taxable if disposal
< 3 years after
subscription

Loss

Always
allowable ■━━━━━━■ Cost figure is reduced
by any EIS IT relief
not withdrawn

Share loss relief
available, so can choose
to set loss against
general income of current
and/or previous year

Seed Enterprise Investment Scheme (SEIS)

Similar to EIS scheme for smaller, early stage companies

Tax reduction of 50% × investment

Max investment = £100,000 a year

Reduction given in the tax year of investment or previous year

Qualifying company

- Carry on new qualifying trade (as for EIS)
- Permanent establishment in the UK
- Unquoted
- Assets ≤ £200,000
- < 25 full-time equivalent employees
- Can only raise up to a lifetime maximum of £150,000
- Not in financial difficulty

If the shares are not retained for at least three years the tax reduction is wholly or partly withdrawn

Notes

- Gains made > 3 years after the share issue are usually exempt from CGT
- Additional CGT exemption for gains reinvested in

Investor

Must not be connected with the company ie, must not:

- Be an employee (although can be a director); or
- Own > 30% of ordinary shares/voting rights

Same reliefs as EIS

- Disposal of SEIS shares
  - Gain exempt if held > 3 years
  - Loss allowable (but cost reduced for any remaining IT relief)
- Share loss relief available

SEIS reinvestment relief

- Gain realised on any asset may be fully or partly exempt if reinvested in SEIS shares in the same year
- Max reinvestment relief = 50% × investment
- Can only carry back reinvestment relief to previous year if also make a carry back claim for IT purposes
- Cannot also claim EIS CGT deferral in respect of same investment
- If IT relief withdrawn, reinvestment relief withdrawn to same extent

  - Max £100,000 investment

Main differences between EIS and SEIS

	EIS	SEIS
Individual		
Investment limit	up to £2 million	£100,000
IT relief	30%	50%
Director investors?	Reasonably paid only	Yes
Reinvestment relief	Deferral	Exemption (max £50,000)
Company		
Max raised investment	£5,000,000 per year	£150,000 total
Gross assets	≤ £15,000,000	≤ £200,000
Employees	< 250/< 500	< 25

Venture Capital Trusts (VCTs)

Investments subscribed for in the ordinary shares of a VCT provide a tax reduction, saving income tax of 30% × investment

VCT

Stock exchange listed company that buys shares in various unlisted (EIS-type) trading companies

Max investment = £200,000 a year

- If the shares are not retained for at least five years the tax reduction is wholly or partly withdrawn

CGT relief

- Capital gain always exempt
- Capital loss not allowable

Dividend exemption

Dividends received from a VCT are exempt from tax

- Provided paid in respect of shares acquired within the permitted maximum investment limit

Notes

3: Employee remuneration

Topic List

Taxable and exempt benefits

Termination payments

Share schemes

Pension schemes

You need to be able to advise on the tax implications of different remuneration packages as well as appropriate structures for termination packages.

You also need to be able to advise on the appropriateness of different share schemes for a given scenario.

Non-cash benefits

- General rule = cost to employer
- Use if no specific rule

Accommodation

Annual value of accommodation is a taxable benefit on **all** employees, unless job-related.

Additional charge if cost (c) more than £75,000:

$$ORI \times (c - £75,000)$$

Use market value if acquired > Six years before provided

Official rate of interest at the start of the tax year

Living expenses

Living expenses connected with accommodation (eg, gas bills) are taxable. However, if the accommodation is job-related, the maximum amount taxable is 10% net earnings

Job-related

- Necessary for proper performance
- For better performance and customary to provide

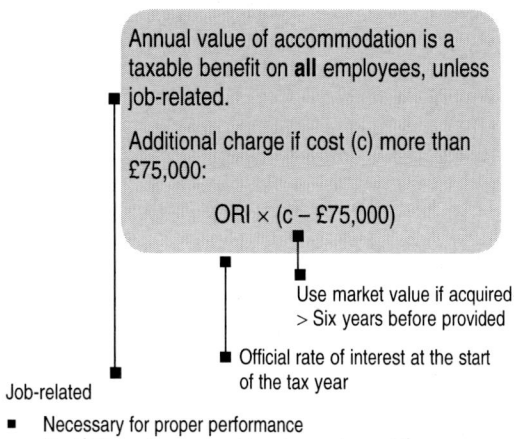

Cars

Depends on car's CO_2 emissions → Max £5,000

Annual taxable benefit for private use of a car is:
(list price of car – capital contributions) × %.
- Refer to tax tables (max is 37%)
- Emissions 1 to 50 g/km % dependent on electric range
- The % increases by 4% for diesel engined cars (max still 37%) unless they meet the RDE2 standard

The benefits are scaled down on a time basis, then the car and van (but **not** fuel) benefits are reduced by any contribution by the employee for private use. ■—— payments to 'make good' by 6 July following the tax year

Vans

Unrestricted private use:
- 0 g/km: £0
- > 0 g/km: £3,600

Fuel benefit:
- > 0 g/km: £688

Fuel – cars

- Fuel for private use is charged as percentage of base figure (£25,300 for 2022/23)
- Same percentage as car benefit
- No reduction for partial reimbursement by the employee

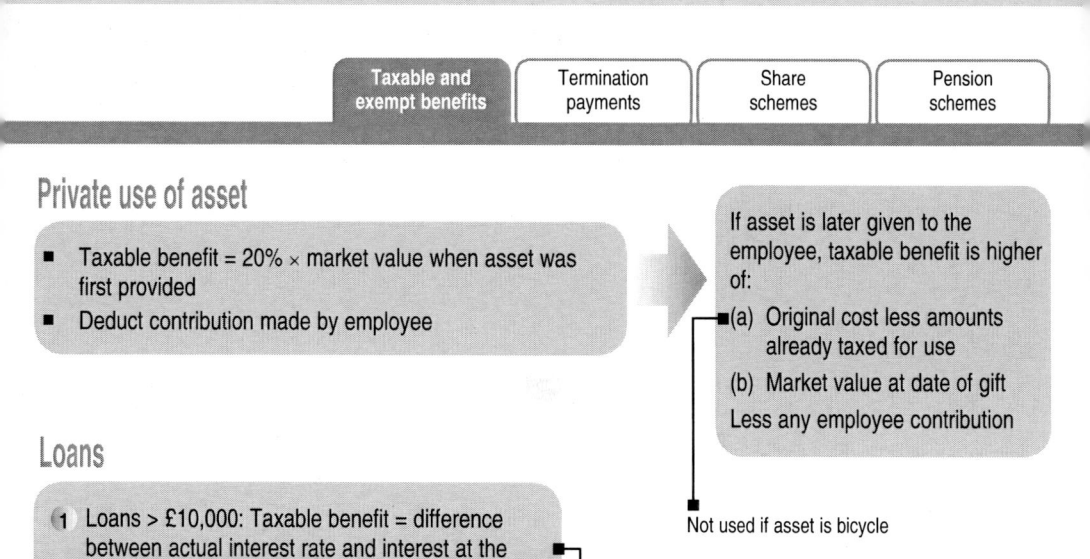

Private use of asset

- Taxable benefit = 20% × market value when asset was first provided
- Deduct contribution made by employee

If asset is later given to the employee, taxable benefit is higher of:

- (a) Original cost less amounts already taxed for use
- (b) Market value at date of gift

Less any employee contribution

Not used if asset is bicycle

Loans

1. Loans > £10,000: Taxable benefit = difference between actual interest rate and interest at the official rate
2. Loan write-off: Taxable benefit = amount written off

Two methods of calculation:
Average balance during tax year × ORI

Exempt benefits

- Loans of up to £10,000
- Meals in staff canteen
- Workplace nurseries
- Job-related accommodation
- Medical insurance for overseas duties
- Mobile phone – restricted to one phone per employee
- Pension contributions to employer's registered scheme
- Relocation expenses of up to £8,000
- Additional household costs for homeworkers

- Up to £6 per week may be claimed without supporting evidence

Expenses

- Include as general earnings
- Deduct if wholly, exclusively and necessarily incurred for performance of duties
- No need to report expense if would be fully allowable as deduction

Salary sacrifice

Taxable value of benefits where salary is sacrificed is higher of:

- Taxable value (using the benefits code); and
- Value of cash sacrificed.

Certain benefits excluded from this (eg, person savings and childcare)

3: Employee remuneration

Termination payments

Termination payments can be a tax efficient method of rewarding employees on the termination of employment.

Tax treatment of termination payments

- **Exempt** → Payments made on death, injury or disability
- **Fully taxable** → Payments to which the employee is contractually entitled
- **Partially exempt** → Ex gratia payments and statutory redundancy pay

Partially exempt

Payments are fully taxable subject to an exemption for the first £30,000

⬇

Taxed in year of receipt (not year when employment terminated)

⬇

Non-cash benefits are valued using the normal benefit rules; some benefits are excluded eg, continued use of mobile phone

⬇

Class 1A NIC payable on payments in excess of £30,000

PILON

- **Post-employment notice pay (PENP)**
  Occurs when employment is terminated during notice period.
  PENP is the basic salary that would have been earned if worked to the end of the notice period.
  PENP is taxable and NICable.

- **Balance of the PILON**

  This is (PILON – PENP)
  It is part of the termination payment subject to

Share option schemes – employees' tax liabilities ■——■Corporation tax deduction usually available for employer

	Grant	Exercise	Disposal
Tax-advantaged scheme	Not taxable	Not normally taxable	Subject to CGT as normal

Other schemes	No tax for options granted after 1.09.03	Taxed as employment income:
		
		     £
		MV on exercise X
		Cost (X)
		Taxable X
			Capital gain on increase in value of shares since exercise date:
			
			       £
			Proceeds X
			Cost (X)⎤ Equal to
			Amount charged to ⎟ MV @
			income tax on exercise (X)⎦ exercise
			Gain X

3: Employee remuneration

Tax-advantaged schemes summary

	CSOP	EMI	SAVE	SIP
Qualifying employees	■ Key employees only ■ Own ≤ 30%	■ Key employees only ■ Own ≤ 30% ■ Work for substantial amount of time for company	■ Open to all employees ■ No maximum holding	■ Open to all employees ■ No maximum holding ■ Can award free shares based on performance
Max value at grant per employee	■ £30,000	■ £250,000 ■ Reduced if also holds shares under CSOP ■ Max £3m in issue	■ Save £10 – £500 per month ■ Buy out of post-tax income	■ Free = £3,600 pa ■ Partnership = £1,800 pa (max 10% salary) ■ Matching = 2:1 ■ Dividend = from SIP

	CSOP	EMI	SAYE	SIP
Conditions	<ul><li>No discount at grant</li><li>Exercisable between 3 and 10 years</li></ul>	<ul><li>May issue at a discount</li><li>Exercisable ≤ 10 years</li><li>Trading company</li><li>Gross assets ≤ £30m</li><li>Quoted or unquoted</li><li>< 250 employees</li></ul>	Maximum 20% discount	<ul><li>Hold for at least three years</li><li>Except partnership shares</li></ul>
Tax treatment at grant	No IT/NIC	No IT/NIC	No IT/NIC	<ul><li>Free = No IT/NIC</li><li>Partnership = Buy out of pre-tax income</li><li>Matching = No IT/NIC</li><li>Dividend = No IT on dividends used to buy more dividend shares</li></ul>

	CSOP	EMI	SAVE	SIP
Tax treatment at exercise	No IT/NIC	Taxable employment income if issued at discount: £ MV @ grant X Exercise price (X) Taxable X Use MV @ exercise (not grant) if lower result	No IT/NIC	N/A
Tax treatment at disposal	Normal CGT: £ Proceeds X Exercise price (X) Taxable X	Normal CGT: £ Proceeds X Exercise price (X) Taxable at exercise (X) Taxable X ■	Normal CGT: £ Proceeds X Exercise price (X) Taxable X	■ Still employee: No CGT ■ Not employee: Normal CGT £ Proceeds X MV when left plan (X) Taxable X

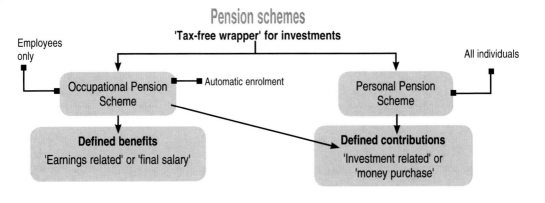

Pension schemes

'Tax-free wrapper' for investments

Employees only

All individuals

Occupational Pension Scheme — Automatic enrolment

Personal Pension Scheme

Defined benefits

'Earnings related' or 'final salary'

Defined contributions

'Investment related' or 'money purchase'

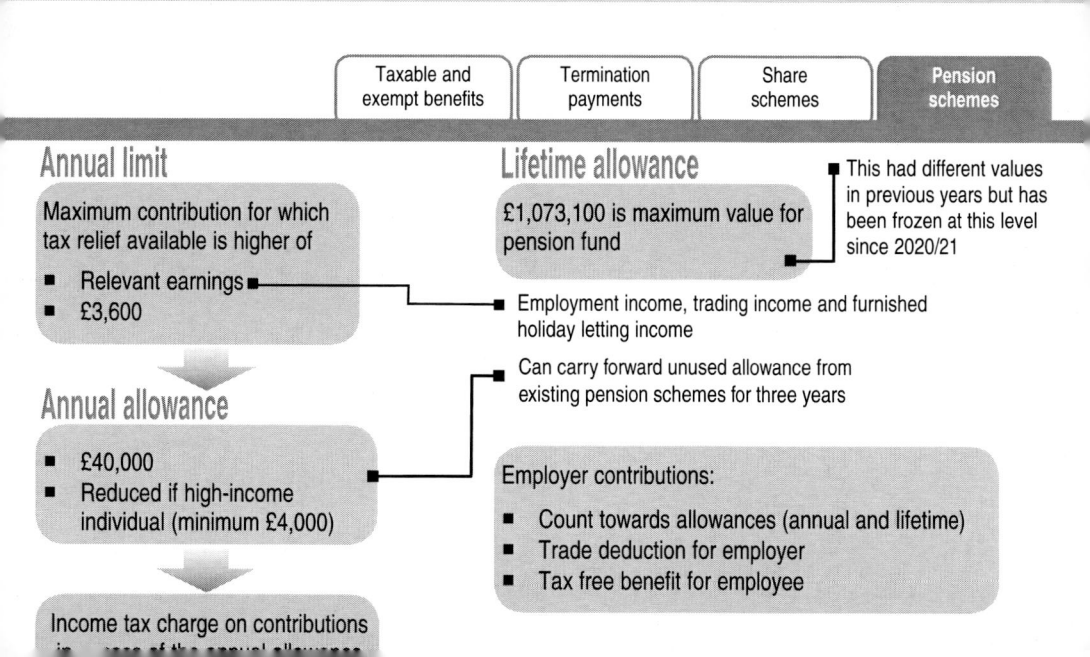

Annual limit

Maximum contribution for which tax relief available is higher of

- Relevant earnings
- £3,600

Annual allowance

- £40,000
- Reduced if high-income individual (minimum £4,000)

Income tax charge on contributions in ~~excess of the annual allowance~~

Lifetime allowance

£1,073,100 is maximum value for pension fund

- This had different values in previous years but has been frozen at this level since 2020/21

Employment income, trading income and furnished holiday letting income

Can carry forward unused allowance from existing pension schemes for three years

Employer contributions:

- Count towards allowances (annual and lifetime)
- Trade deduction for employer
- Tax free benefit for employee

Tax relief

```
┌──────────────────┐          ┌──────────────────┐
│   Occupational   │          │     Personal     │
│     pension      │          │     pension      │
└──────────────────┘          └──────────────────┘
         │                             │
         ▼                             ▼
```

Deduct gross employee contributions directly from employment income in the income tax computation

- Paid net so automatic 20% tax relief
- Higher/additional rate taxpayers extend basic and higher rate tax bands by gross contributions

ie, payment × 100/80

- This is the same method of giving tax relief as for Gift Aid donations

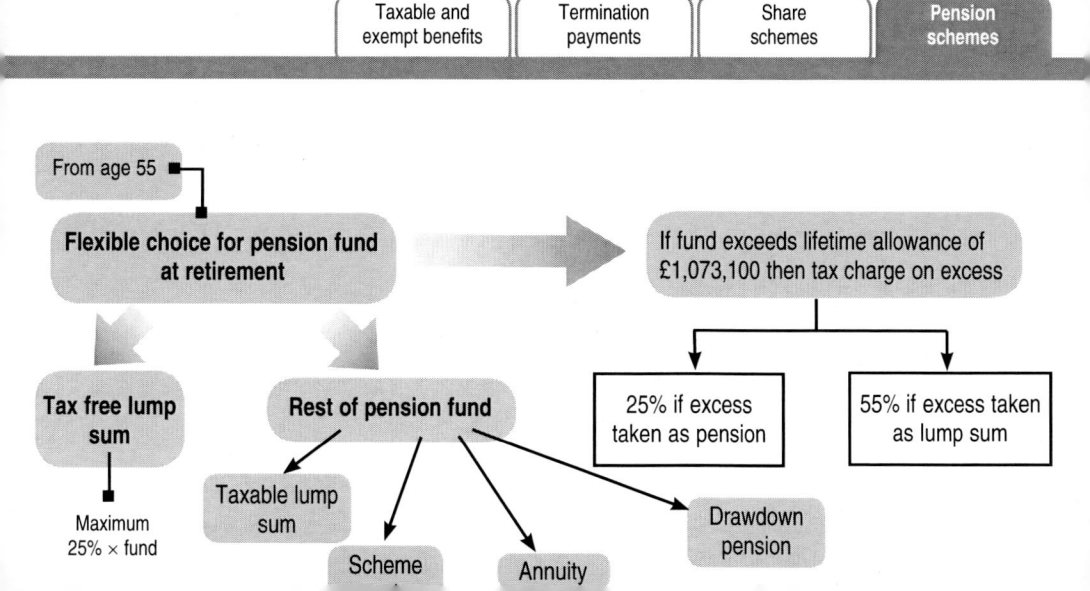

4: Unincorporated businesses

Topic List

Revision from Tax Compliance – calculation of trading profit/loss

Revision from Tax Compliance – relief for trading losses

Choice of loss relief

This chapter revises the rules you learned for your Tax Compliance exam. You need to be able to calculate the trading proft or loss, and identify the trading loss relief options for new businesses, businesses that have been trading a while, and those ceasing to trade or being incorporated.

Calculating the individual's taxable income after losses are relieved is also key, along with giving recommendations.

Adjustment of profits

To arrive at taxable trading profits, the net accounts profit must be adjusted.

- Certain items of expenditure are not deductible (ie, not allowable) for trading income purposes and must be added back to the net accounts profit when computing trading profits.
- Conversely other items are deductible (ie, **allowable**).

Allowable expenditure

Expenditure incurred **wholly** and **exclusively** for trade purposes

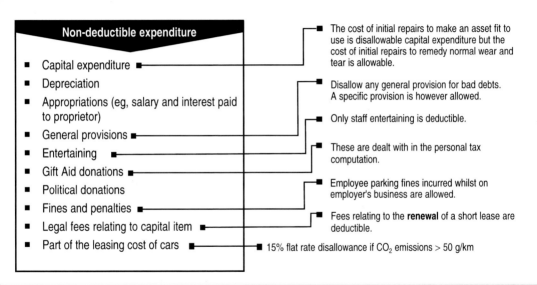

Non-deductible expenditure

- Capital expenditure
- Depreciation
- Appropriations (eg, salary and interest paid to proprietor)
- General provisions
- Entertaining
- Gift Aid donations
- Political donations
- Fines and penalties
- Legal fees relating to capital item
- Part of the leasing cost of cars

- The cost of initial repairs to make an asset fit to use is disallowable capital expenditure but the cost of initial repairs to remedy normal wear and tear is allowable.

- Disallow any general provision for bad debts. A specific provision is however allowed.

- Only staff entertaining is deductible.

- These are dealt with in the personal tax computation.

- Employee parking fines incurred whilst on employer's business are allowed.

- Fees relating to the **renewal** of a short lease are deductible.

- 15% flat rate disallowance if CO_2 emissions > 50 g/km

Other adjustments

Trading profits not shown in the accounts must be **added** ■━━━■ Eg, business owner takes goods for own use without reimbursing full market value, or receives payment in non-money form without including money's worth in accounts

Non-trading income in the accounts must be **removed** ■━━━■ Eg, rental income, profits on the disposal of fixed assets and investment income

Expenditure not shown in the accounts must be **deducted** ■━━━■ Eg, business expenditure paid personally by the owner

Pre-trading expenditure

Deductible on first day of trading providing:

- Incurred in the seven years prior to commencement of trade
- Would have been deductible trading expenditure if incurred after trade commenced

Fixed rate expenses

■ Can also choose to be taxed on the cash basis

Certain small businesses can, instead of actual expenses, deduct fixed rate amounts for:

- Motor vehicles
- Use of home for business purposes
- Business premises partly used as home

Current year basis (CYB)

> The basis period for a tax year is normally the period of account ending in the year.

There are special rules which apply in the opening and closing years of a business

Opening years

Any profits taxed twice as a result of these rules = **'overlap profits'**

Relieved when:

- Business ends
- Change of accounting date

Tax year	Basis period
1	**'Actual basis':** Date of commencement to following 5 April
2	Depends on length of accounting period ending in year 2: (a) 12 months: tax that 12 months (b) < 12 months: tax the 1st 12 months of trade (c) >12 months: tax the 12 months up to the accounting date (d) No accounting date ends in year: 6 April–5 April ('actual' basis)
3	12 months to accounting date ending in year

Closing year ──── Tax year that trade ends

- Basis period for the final year starts at the end of the basis period for the previous year and ends at cessation.
- Any overlap profits not already relieved are deducted from the final year's profits.

> - If business ends in 1st tax year, tax all the profits
> - If business ends in 2nd tax year, tax from 6 April until business ends

NOTE: Basis periods will be abolished from 2024/25 (transition period 2023/24); therefore, basis period

Capital allowances plant & machinery

Main pool

The main pool contains:

- All machinery, fixtures, fittings, equipment
- Vans, forklift trucks, lorries, motorcycles
- Cars with CO_2 emissions $\leq$ 50 g/km

Writing down allowances (WDAs)

Balance = **tax written down value (TWDV)**

- 18% per annum on a reducing balance basis
- 18% $\times$ months/12 in a period that is not 12 months long
- Can claim less CAs than maximum possible

4: Unincorporated businesses

First year allowances (FYAs)

- Replace WDAs in period of expenditure
- **Not pro-rated in short/long accounting periods**
- Not usually available on cars

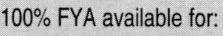

100% FYA available for:
- **New** zero emission cars
- **New** zero emission goods vehicles
- Qualifying R+D capital expenditure
- Expenditure by **companies** in a designated enterprise zone
- Electric vehicle charging point

Annual Investment Allowance (AIA)

- For all businesses for expenditure up to £1 million pa until 31 March 2023 and £200k pa from 1 April 2023 onwards.
- For AP straddling 31 March 2023 the AIA is calculated pro rata, but the max expenditure eligible after 31 March 2023 is £200,000 pro-rated for months post 31 March 2023
- Scaled up/down for long/short accounting periods of account
- Allocate AIA to assets eligible for **lowest** rate of WDA
- Balance of expenditure after AIA receives WDA

- Expected economic working life 25+ years
- Expenditure >£100,000 in period (pro rate for periods <12m)

Special rate pool

Expenditure on:
- Long life assets (LLAs)
- Integral features
- Thermal insulation and solar panels
- Cars with CO_2 emissions >50 g/km

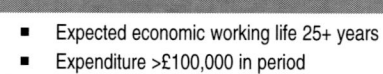

- WDA = 6% per annum on reducing balance basis
- Given after AIA if available
- Pro rate in a period that is not 12 months long

WDA for small pools

- If balance on main/special rate pool < small pool limit at end of chargeable period, can claim WDA up to small pool limit
- Small pool limit = £1,000 for 12 month chargeable period
- Pro rate for short/long periods

- Electrical systems
- Cold water systems
- Ventilation systems
- Lifts
- Escalators

Private use assets ■─■ Assets used privately by the owner **not** an employee

- Keep each asset used privately by the business owner in a separate 'pool'
- AIA, FYA and WDA are calculated in full and deducted to calculate TWDV
- **But** can only claim the **business** proportion of allowances

Otherwise ■ TWDV must be transferred to main pool

Short life assets (SLA)

Not cars/assets with private use

- An **election** can be made to **depool** main pool assets
- Depooled assets must be disposed of within **eight years** of end of the period of acquisition
- From a planning point of view depooling is useful if balancing allowances are expected

Pre-trading expenditure

- Eligible for capital allowances
- Treated as incurred on first day of trading

Cars – summary

- Cars with CO_2 emissions > 50 g/km
  - Special rate pool
  - WDA 6% per annum
- Cars with CO_2 emissions ≤ 50 g/km
  - Main pool
  - WDA 18% per annum
- FYA for zero emission car
- No AIA for cars

If private use asset, use CO_2 emissions to determine rate of WDA then apply private use asset rules

Balancing adjustments arise

| On cessation to deal with balances remaining after deduction of disposal proceeds | When a non-pooled asset is sold | When a column balance becomes negative |

- No WDAs/FYAs/AIAs on cessation

Successions

This will be a balancing charge (increases profits)

- If trade is transferred to a connected person assets transfer at TWDV, so no balancing adjustments
- No WDAs, FYAs or AIAs in the period of disposal for the old owner; only WDAs for the new owner on the assets transferred

Balancing allowances

- Only arise in the main and special rate pools when trade ends

By joint election

Eg, – Incorporation
 – Transfer to close relative

Structures and buildings allowance (SBA)

Eligible construction costs of new non-residential structures and buildings

- Construction of building (excl. land)
- Renovation or conversion of building
- Cost of new asset purchased from the developer (excl. land)

Allowances

$$SBA = Cost \times 3\% \text{ pa}$$

- From later of first use and expenditure
- Addition to building starts a new 33 1/3 year period for that new cost
- SBA apportioned for periods of less than or more than 12 months
- No balancing adjustment on sale (apportion allowances between vendor and purchaser)
- Any SBAs claimed added to sale proceeds in capital

Calculation of loss

Calculate trading income in the normal way. If it is negative then that amount is the loss for the year and taxable trading income is nil.

Alert! Losses in two overlapping basis periods are treated as losses of the earlier tax year only. Do **not** double count the losses.

Example

Sue starts trading on 1.10.21. Her losses are:
y/e 30.9.22 £(50,000)
y/e 30.9.23 £(20,000)

Losses for the tax years are:

2021/22
1.10.21–5.4.22 £(25,000)

2022/23
y/e 30.9.22 £(25,000) ie, £(50,000 – 25,000)

First 12 months less the losses allocated to 2021/22

Carry forward (s.83)

A loss not otherwise relieved may be set against the first available profits of the same trade.

Losses **must** be set against the first available profits: they cannot be saved up until it suits the trader to use them

Losses may be carried forward for any number of years but if the trade changes, there is no further relief

Consideration for the sale of the business must be wholly or mainly shares (80%)

Incorporation (s.86)

When a business is transferred to a company (ie, incorporated), pre-incorporation losses can be carried forward by the trader (not by the company) against the first available income they receive from the company.

Relief against general income (s.64)

Relief is against the general income of the tax year of the loss and/or the preceding tax year.

- Partial claims are not allowed: the whole loss must be set off, if there is income to absorb it in the chosen tax year.
- The trade must be carried on on a commercial basis with a view to the realisation of profits.

If claim against general income made can extend the claim to net chargeable gains of the same tax year, less brought forward capital losses.

Opening years (s.72)

A loss incurred:

- In the first **four** tax years of trade can be set against
- **Total income** of the **three** preceding tax years

Relief is given in the earlier year first (FIFO)

Include unrelieved overlap profits

If (a) or (b) yield a profit, assume the figure is nil.

Closing years (s.89)

A loss incurred in:

- The last **12 months** of trade can be set against **trading profits** in
- The year of cessation and in the **three** preceding tax years

Relief is given in the later years first (LIFO)

Computation of terminal loss

	£
(a) Actual trading loss for tax year of cessation (6 April to date of cessation)	X
(b) Actual trading loss for period from 12 months before cessation to 5 April	X
	X
Terminal loss	X

Summary	s.83	s.64	s.72	s.89
Type of loss relief	CF	CY and/or PY (any order)	Loss in 1st 4 tax years	Terminal loss relief on cessation
Set against	Future trading profits from same trade	Total income	Total income	Trading profits from same trade
Time limits	CF until fully utilised or cease to trade	CY and/or PY	CB to previous 3 years on FIFO basis	CB to previous 3 years on LIFO basis
Conditions	■ Automatic ■ Cannot restrict to preserve PA	■ Optional ■ All or nothing ■ Claim in 1 or both years (any order)	■ Optional ■ All or nothing	■ Optional ■ All or nothing
Claim	Agree amount of loss within 4 years of end of tax year of loss	Within 12 months from 31 January following end of tax year of loss	Within 12 months from 31 January following end of tax year of loss	Within 4 years of end of last tax year in which business operated

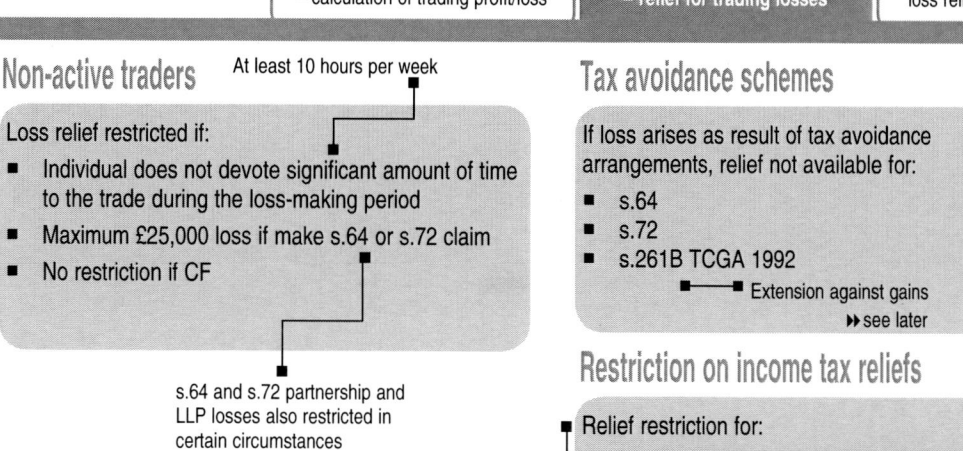

Non-active traders

At least 10 hours per week

Loss relief restricted if:

- Individual does not devote significant amount of time to the trade during the loss-making period
- Maximum £25,000 loss if make s.64 or s.72 claim
- No restriction if CF

s.64 and s.72 partnership and LLP losses also restricted in certain circumstances

Limited to higher of:
- £50,000

Tax avoidance schemes

If loss arises as result of tax avoidance arrangements, relief not available for:

- s.64
- s.72
- s.261B TCGA 1992

Extension against gains
▶▶ see later

Restriction on income tax reliefs

Relief restriction for:

- Trading losses and property losses set against total income
- Interest on loan to invest in close company

Considerations

- Income tax rate in relevant tax years
- Potential waste of loss where net income already covered by PA
- Potential waste of PA to achieve higher rate tax savings
- Projected level of future profits and tax rates

■ Also type of income eg, are dividends covered by the dividend nil rate band?

Notes

5: Capital gains tax

You must be able to calculate gains as part of a personal tax question, often setting off gains and losses.

You should also be able to identify the option for relieving trading income losses against gains, and calculate the optimum form of loss relief.

You must also be able to advise an individual of capital gains tax planning opportunities within the family unit.

Chargeable persons, assets and disposals

Three elements are needed for a chargeable gain to arise.

1 A **chargeable person**: companies, individuals, partners and trustees are chargeable persons. ■——————■ Charities and pension schemes are exempt from CGT

2 A **chargeable asset**: most assets wherever situated in the world are chargeable, but some assets are exempt. ■
- Cars
- Some chattels (eg, racehorses)
- Gilts
- ISA investments

3 A **chargeable disposal**: this includes sales and gifts. Transfer of assets on death is not chargeable.

Computation

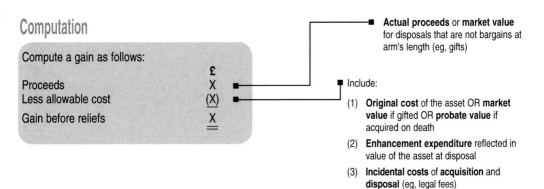

Compute a gain as follows:

	£
Proceeds	X
Less allowable cost	(X)
Gain before reliefs	X

- **Actual proceeds** or **market value** for disposals that are not bargains at arm's length (eg, gifts)

- Include:

  (1) **Original cost** of the asset OR **market value** if gifted OR **probate value** if acquired on death

  (2) **Enhancement expenditure** reflected in value of the asset at disposal

  (3) **Incidental costs** of **acquisition** and **disposal** (eg, legal fees)

Part disposals

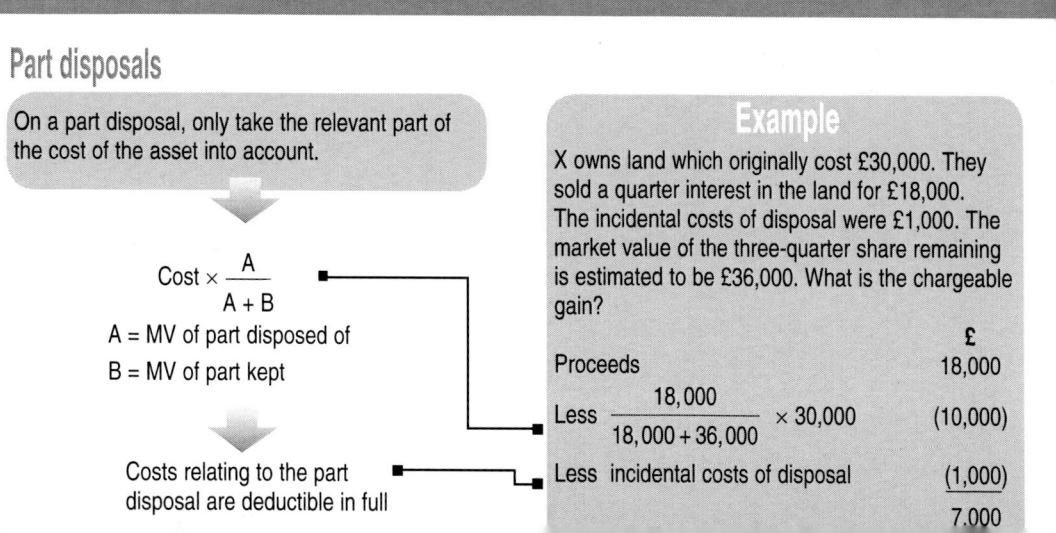

On a part disposal, only take the relevant part of the cost of the asset into account.

$$\text{Cost} \times \frac{A}{A + B}$$

A = MV of part disposed of

B = MV of part kept

Costs relating to the part disposal are deductible in full

Example

X owns land which originally cost £30,000. They sold a quarter interest in the land for £18,000. The incidental costs of disposal were £1,000. The market value of the three-quarter share remaining is estimated to be £36,000. What is the chargeable gain?

	£
Proceeds	18,000
Less $\dfrac{18,000}{18,000 + 36,000} \times 30,000$	(10,000)
Less incidental costs of disposal	(1,000)
	7,000

Spouses/civil partners

Transfers between them take place at no gain/no loss
ie, proceeds = cost

Connected persons

- Transfers between connected persons (**relatives,
  business partners, settlor of a trust and its
  trustees**) take place at market value

Trustees are also
connected to anyone
connected with the settlor

Deduct allowable capital losses from chargeable gains in the tax year in which they arise.

Any loss that cannot be set off is carried forward to set against future chargeable gains.

The net gains for the year are reduced by the annual exempt amount before then deducting any allowable losses brought forward.

Except losses on disposals to connected persons:

- Set only against gains on transfers to **same** person
- In same or future years

Capital losses on disposal of qualifying shares (EIS/SEIS or unquoted trading companies) may be offset against individual's net income for current

Example

Zoë made chargeable gains of £14,000 in 2022/23. She had brought forward capital losses of £8,000.

The AEA of £12,300 reduces the gain to £1,700 allowing £1,700 of the brought forward capital loss to be set off in 2022/23. The remaining loss will be carried forward to 2023/24

Annual exempt amount (AEA)

Individuals

- £12,300 (2022/23)

Trustees

- £6,150 (2022/23)
- Split between all trusts set up by same settlor

Minimum = £1,230 (2022/23)

Rates of CGT

Individuals

	Residential property	Other assets
Within BRB	18%	10%
Above BRB	28%	20%

Trustees

Residential property	Other assets
28%	20%

Extend BRB by:
- Gross Gift Aid donations
- Gross personal pension contributions

Business asset disposal relief ▶▶ See Chapter 6

- Reduces CGT payable on certain **qualifying business disposals**
- Gains qualifying for relief taxed at 10%
- Deduct losses and AEA so taxpayer pays least amount of tax

- Residential property gains first
- Then, other non-BADR gains
- Then BADR gains
- **But** BADR gains use up BRB in priority to non-BADR gains

Relief for trading losses against gains (s.261B)

Claim to set loss against the general income of:

- The tax year of the loss; and/or
- The preceding tax year

- Can extend the claim for unrelieved part of the loss
- Set against chargeable gains of the same tax year as income tax claim

Available loss is **lower** of :

- 'Relevant' amount ie, unrelieved trading loss

- 'Maximum' amount ie:

Ignore AEA for these purposes

	£
CY capital gain	X
Less CY capital losses	(X)
Less capital losses b/f	(X)

Deferred consideration

Payable in instalments

- Ignore fact that paid in instalments
- Tax full proceeds in tax year of disposal
- Can pay tax in instalments if instalment period >18m

Future payment conditional and known

- Ignore fact that consideration is conditional
- Include future proceeds in tax year of disposal
- If conditions not met in future, amend computation

Future payment conditional but unknown

- Proceeds include:
  - Actual proceeds received, and
  - Estimated net present value (NPV) of **right to receive the rest**
- Receipt of future consideration is a disposal of that 'earn out' right
- Cost = original NPV
- If amount received < NPV, can carry back the loss arising

'Earn out'

Individuals only

Notes

6: Capital gains tax – reliefs

Topic List

Revision from Tax Compliance

Incorporation relief

Takeovers and reconstructions

In advising businesses of their taxable gains you will be required to identify when business asset disposal relief, rollover relief, gift relief or incorporation relief apply.

You also need to be able to calculate the reliefs where specific restrictions apply, for example some non-business use for rollover relief.

Rollover relief

Taxpayers can claim to defer gains arising on the disposal of business assets that are being replaced if both the old and the new assets are on the list of eligible assets.

> The new asset must be bought in the period starting **12 months before** and ending **36 months after** the disposal.

Exam focus

If a question mentions the sale of some business assets and the purchase of others, look out for rollover relief but do not just assume that it is available: the assets might be of the wrong type eg, moveable plant and machinery.

Eligible assets

- Land and buildings (including parts of buildings) occupied as well as used only for the purposes of the trade
- Fixed (that is, immoveable) plant and machinery
- Goodwill (individuals only)

A depreciating asset is one with an expected life of 60 years or less (eg, fixed plant and machinery).

Is the new asset a **depreciating** asset?
Is the new asset a **non-depreciating** asset?

For a **non-depreciating asset** the gain is **deducted from the base cost of the new asset**.

For a **depreciating asset** the **gain is deferred** until it crystallises at a later date.

The gain crystallises on the earliest of:

1. The disposal of the replacement asset

2. 10 years after the acquisition of the replacement asset

3. The date the replacement asset ceases to be used in the trade

If a part of the proceeds of the old asset are not reinvested, the gain is chargeable up to the amount not reinvested.

Non-business use

Relief is proportionately restricted when an asset has not been used for trade purposes throughout its life.

If a non-depreciating qualifying asset is bought before the gain crystallises, the deferred gain may be rolled into the base cost of that asset.

Alert! If any gain remains after rollover relief, business asset disposal relief may apply.

Gift relief

- Available for outright gifts and sales below market value of **qualifying assets**
- Chargeable gain is **deferred**

Qualifying assets

- Assets used in a trade by donor or donor's personal company
- Shares and securities
  - Unquoted
  - Quoted: must hold $\geq 5\%$ voting rights

- Personal companies' restriction:

$$\text{Gain} \times \frac{\text{CBA}}{\text{CA}}$$

Must be a trading company (HMRC apply a 20% test)

Recipient must be UK resident

Deduct deferred gain from recipient's base cost

Alert! If any gain remains after gift relief, business asset disposal relief may apply

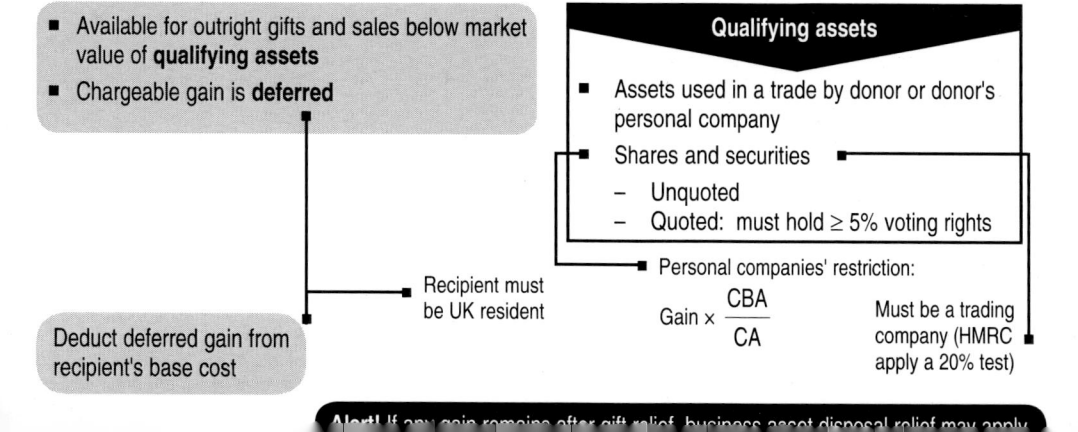

Sales at below MV

Receive actual proceeds but less than market value

Real profit is chargeable ie:

	£
Actual proceeds received	X
Less actual cost	(X)
Gain chargeable now	X

Rest of gain is deferred by gift relief

Deduct this deferred gain from recipient's base cost

Business asset disposal relief

- Reduces CGT payable on certain **qualifying business disposals**
- Lifetime limit: **£1 million**
- Gains qualifying for relief taxed at 10%

Qualifying business disposal

(1) All/part of a trading business as a going concern (includes partnership interests)
(2) Assets which were used for the purposes of a business which has recently ceased
(3) Shares in the individual's personal trading company in which the individual is an employee

Crystallise a gain to get BADR, where no longer a personal company due to a new share issue for cash

Qualifying period of ownership

- Owned business for two years before disposal

- Owned business for two years before cessation and assets disposed of within three years of cessation

- Qualifying conditions must have applied for two years before disposal ■——■ Runs from option **grant** date for EMI shares

- Owns ≥ 5% of ordinary shares, voting rights, profits ■——■ Not required for distribution and assets on a winding up ■——■ for EMI shares

Associated disposals

Disposal of individual business assets owned personally and used in a continuing trade only qualify for relief if:

1 Disposal of **partnership interest or qualifying shares**;

2 Individual makes disposal as part of **withdrawal from participation** in the business; and

3 Throughout a period of two years prior to the disposal the **assets are used for business purposes**.

- eg, building owned personally but used by the partnership/company

if acquired on/after 13 June 2016 must have been owned for three years at disposal

at least 5% interest/ shareholding or entire shareholding if < 5%

Investors' relief

- Subscribe for new shares on/after 17 March 2016 — No minimum shareholding
- Unlisted trading company — Must not work for the company
- Held continually for three years before disposal

Private residence relief

Exempts gain on disposal of a private residence for periods of actual and deemed occupation as proportion of total ownership

Deemed occupation
■ Last nine months
■ Up to three years for any reason ■
■ Any period where individual was required by ■ employment to live abroad
■ Up to four years where individual was required ■ to live elsewhere due to work

■ Must be preceded and followed by actual occupation unless prevented from returning by reasons of employment

Letting relief

Partial exemption of gain where individual lets out part of main residence as residential accommodation (therefore not exempt under PRR) and the owner continues to share occupation. Lower of:

■ Gain during let period
■ PRR
■ £40,000

Incorporation relief

Relief applies when a sole trader or partnership sells/transfers their business to a company.

Applies automatically but can be disapplied by election.

Business must be transferred as a going concern.

All of the assets (or all except cash) must be transferred to the company.

The consideration must be at least partly shares.

Alert! If any gain remains after incorporation relief, business asset disposal relief may apply (except for gain on goodwill transferred to a close company if owns $\geq 5\%$ shareholding).

The gain is deducted from the base cost of the shares instead of being immediately chargeable.

If only a proportion of the consideration is in the form of shares, relief is restricted to that proportion of the gain.

	Rollover relief	**Gift relief**
How does it work?	■ Sell asset and acquire replacement ■ Both used in trade ■ Reinvest in 12m before or 36m after disposal	■ Gift qualifying asset
What qualifies?	■ Land and buildings ■ Goodwill ■ Fixed plant and fixed machinery	■ Business asset ■ Any unquoted trading co shares ■ > 5% quoted trading co shares
How much is the relief?	■ Whole gain if all proceeds reinvested ■ Otherwise proceeds not reinvested = chargeable	■ Whole gain if no cash received ■ Otherwise actual gain = chargeable ■ CBA/CA restriction for shares
How is relief given?	■ Non-depreciating: gain reduces new asset's base cost ■ Depreciating: gain held over (max 10 years)	■ Gain reduces donee's base cost

	Incorporation relief	Business asset disposal/Investors' relief
How does it work?	■ Transfer all business's assets except cash to limited company in return for shares	■ 10% CGT rate always applies
What qualifies?	■ Business assets if all transferred as a going concern	Business asset disposal relief: ■ Unincorporated business sale ■ Sale of shares in trading co if (a) 5% holding and (b) employee ■ Owned for two years Investors' relief: ■ Non-employee shareholders ■ Unlisted, trading company ■ Held > three years
How much is the relief?	■ Whole gain if no cash received ■ Otherwise gain relating to cash is immediately chargeable	■ Lifetime limit of £1m for Business asset disposal relief and £10m for Investors' relief eligible for 10% rate ■ Separate limit for each relief
How is relief given?	■ Gain reduces base cost of shares received	■ **Not** a deferral ■ Always tax gain at 10%

Interaction of reliefs

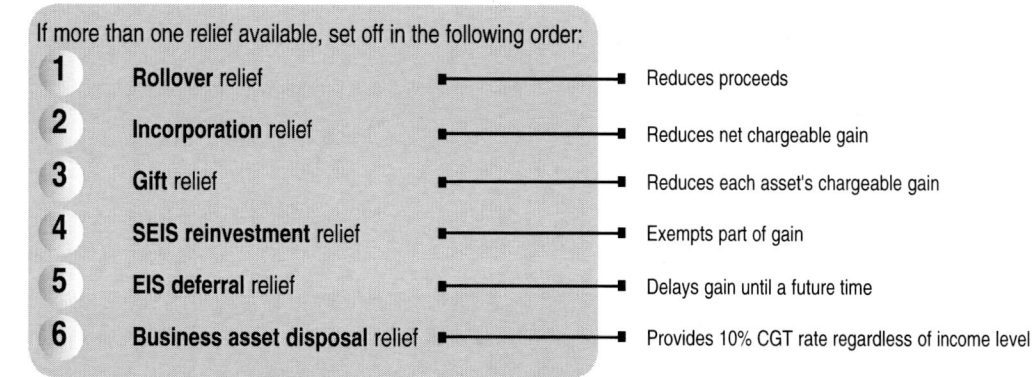

If more than one relief available, set off in the following order:

1   **Rollover** relief   ■————————■ Reduces proceeds

2   **Incorporation** relief   ■————————■ Reduces net chargeable gain

3   **Gift** relief   ■————————■ Reduces each asset's chargeable gain

4   **SEIS reinvestment** relief   ■————————■ Exempts part of gain

5   **EIS deferral** relief   ■————————■ Delays gain until a future time

6   **Business asset disposal** relief   ■————————■ Provides 10% CGT rate regardless of income level

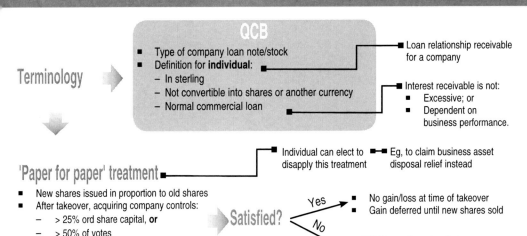

Terminology

QCB

- Type of company loan note/stock
- Definition for **individual**:
  - In sterling
  - Not convertible into shares or another currency
  - Normal commercial loan

■ Loan relationship receivable for a company

■ Interest receivable is not:
  - Excessive; or
  - Dependent on business performance.

'Paper for paper' treatment

■ Individual can elect to disapply this treatment ■─■ Eg, to claim business asset disposal relief instead

- New shares issued in proportion to old shares
- After takeover, acquiring company controls:
  - > 25% ord share capital, **or**
  - > 50% of votes
- Not part of tax avoidance scheme

Satisfied?

Yes →
- No gain/loss at time of takeover
- Gain deferred until new shares sold

No →
- HMRC can disapply relief
- Normal disposal by shareholder
- Immediate gain/loss

Reorganisations and takeovers

→ **Shares received in exchange for shares**

　　└ Same rules apply for non-QCB loan stock

- **'Paper for paper'**
- No gain/loss
- New holding deemed acquired on same date and at same cost as original holding

→ **Shares and cash received**

　　Proceeds = cash received

- Part disposal for cash element
- No gain for shares received
- Split base cost between cash (A) and shares (B) using: $\dfrac{A}{A+B}$

→ **Qualifying corporate bond (QCB) received**

- No gain for QCB element received
- **But** calculate gain and freeze it
- Charge frozen gain when QCBs disposed of

7: Inheritance tax

Topic List

This chapter covers how to advise on the use of business property relief in tax planning strategies for different individuals.

It also deals with HMRC's approach to gifts made with reservation of benefit and shows you how an individual's inheritance tax payable on death may be reduced by using a deed of variation.

You must also be able to identify when gift relief is available on lifetime transfers.

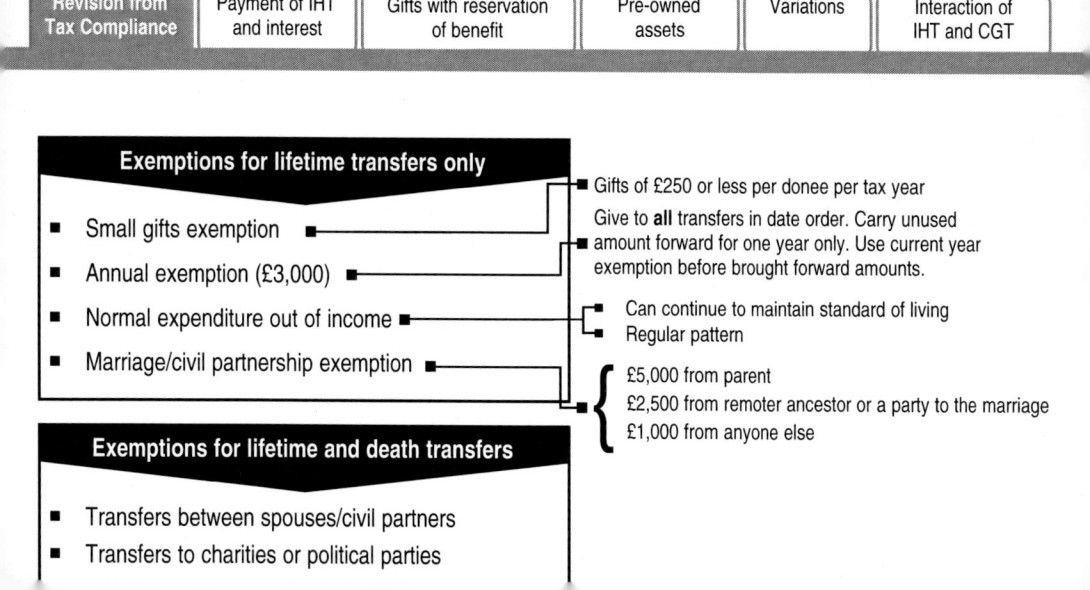

Exemptions for lifetime transfers only

- Small gifts exemption ■ ── Gifts of £250 or less per donee per tax year
- Annual exemption (£3,000) ■ ── Give to **all** transfers in date order. Carry unused amount forward for one year only. Use current year exemption before brought forward amounts.
- Normal expenditure out of income ■ ── Can continue to maintain standard of living / Regular pattern
- Marriage/civil partnership exemption ■ ── £5,000 from parent / £2,500 from remoter ancestor or a party to the marriage / £1,000 from anyone else

Exemptions for lifetime and death transfers

- Transfers between spouses/civil partners
- Transfers to charities or political parties

Assets are generally valued at their open market values.

Diminution in value

Value before transfer	X
Value left with after transfer	(X)
Transfer of value	X

Related property

Related property includes:

1 Property owned by the transferor's spouse
2 Property which the transferor or their spouse gave to a charity or political party in an exempt transfer, if the recipient has owned the property within the preceding five years

Related property is taken into account if doing so increases the value of assets

Special valuation rules

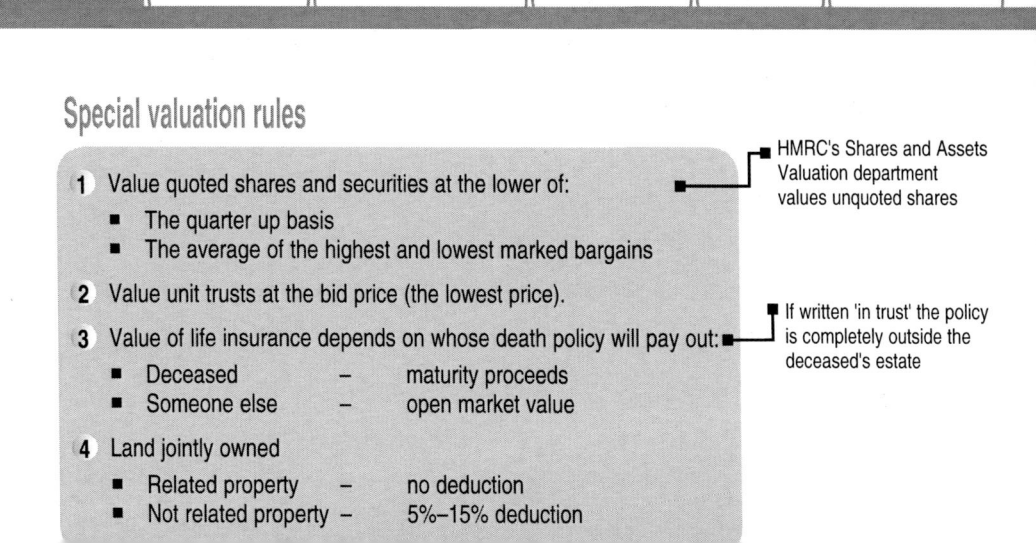

1. Value quoted shares and securities at the lower of:
   - The quarter up basis
   - The average of the highest and lowest marked bargains

   ■ HMRC's Shares and Assets Valuation department values unquoted shares

2. Value unit trusts at the bid price (the lowest price).

3. Value of life insurance depends on whose death policy will pay out:

   ■ If written 'in trust' the policy is completely outside the deceased's estate

   - Deceased   –   maturity proceeds
   - Someone else –   open market value

4. Land jointly owned
   - Related property   –   no deduction
   - Not related property –   5%–15% deduction

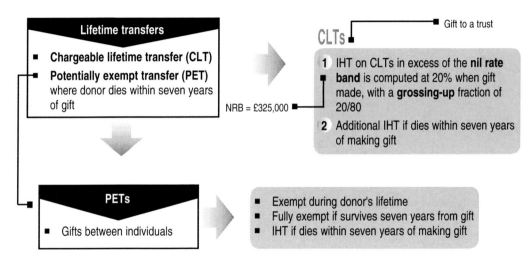

Lifetime transfers

- **Chargeable lifetime transfer (CLT)**
- **Potentially exempt transfer (PET)**
  where donor dies within seven years
  of gift

NRB = £325,000

CLTs ■━━━━━━━━━━━━━━ ■ Gift to a trust

1 IHT on CLTs in excess of the **nil rate band** is computed at 20% when gift made, with a **grossing-up** fraction of 20/80

2 Additional IHT if dies within seven years of making gift

PETs

- Gifts between individuals

- Exempt during donor's lifetime
- Fully exempt if survives seven years from gift
- IHT if dies within seven years of making gift

Additional tax due on death

The IHT on each **lifetime transfer** made in the seven years before death is found as follows:

1. All chargeable transfers (including **PETs** which have become chargeable) in the seven years before the transfer in question use up the nil rate band.
2. Find the tax at full rates (0% and 40%), then deduct any taper relief.
3. Deduct any tax already paid on the transfer (CLTs only – no repayment available).

- Transfers remain in the cumulation and use the nil band for seven years, then they drop out

- A % reduction in the IHT charge is given if the transfer was made more than three years before death

Fall in value relief

If at date of donor's death a gifted asset has either:

1 Been sold for less than its MV when originally gifted

or

2 Is still held but is worth less than its MV when originally gifted

Deduct 'fall in value' from gross chargeable transfer (GCT)

Alert! Fall in value relief only affects the calculation of tax for the donee. It does **not** affect the donor's cumulative total.

Calculating death tax

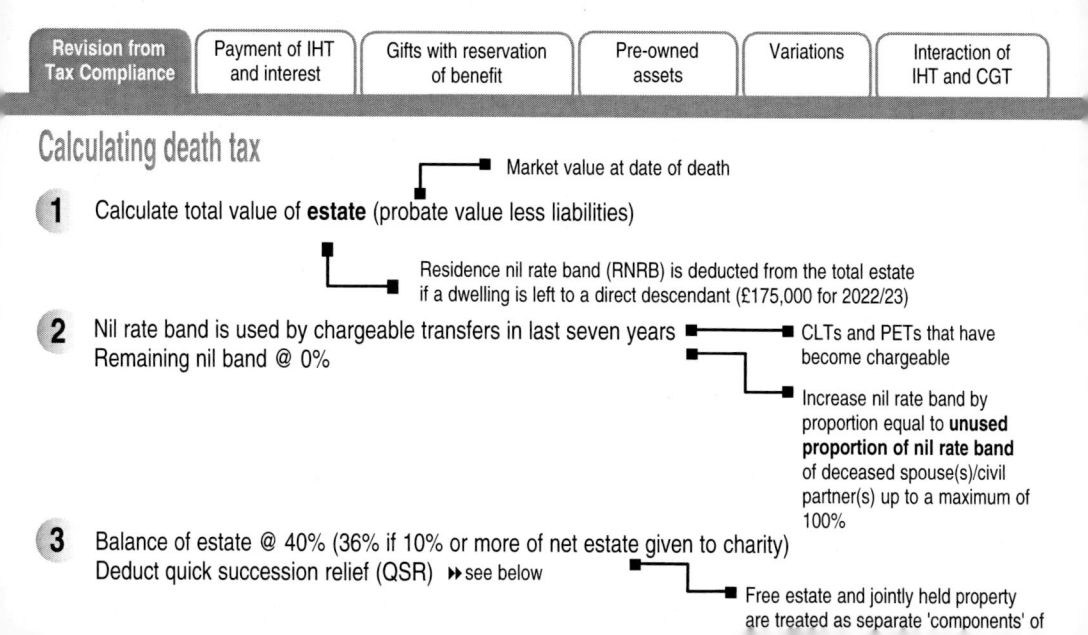

Market value at date of death

1 Calculate total value of **estate** (probate value less liabilities)

Residence nil rate band (RNRB) is deducted from the total estate if a dwelling is left to a direct descendant (£175,000 for 2022/23)

2 Nil rate band is used by chargeable transfers in last seven years
Remaining nil band @ 0%

CLTs and PETs that have become chargeable

Increase nil rate band by proportion equal to **unused proportion of nil rate band** of deceased spouse(s)/civil partner(s) up to a maximum of 100%

3 Balance of estate @ 40% (36% if 10% or more of net estate given to charity)
Deduct quick succession relief (QSR) ▸ see below

Free estate and jointly held property are treated as separate 'components' of

Quick succession relief (QSR)

QSR is given when someone dies within five years of receiving property in a chargeable transfer (the first transfer).

QSR is deducted from the IHT on the estate.

Computation

1. Take the tax paid on the first transfer, and multiply it by the net transfer/the gross transfer.

2. Then multiply the result by a percentage, from 100% (for a gap of one year or less) to 20% (for a gap of more than four years).

Period between transfers	% relief
1 yr or less	100
1–2 yrs	80
2–3 yrs	60
3–4 yrs	40
4–5 yrs	20
> 5 yrs	0

Deemed domicile

Treat as UK domiciled for IHT:

- If resident in the UK for 15 out of previous 20 tax years
- A 'formerly domiciled resident'

- Born in the UK
- UK domicile of origin
- UK resident in tax year of transfer
- UK resident in one of two previous tax years

- UK domiciled – IHT on all assets wherever situated
- Non-UK domiciled – IHT only on UK assets

Double tax relief

DTR is available if property is situated overseas and suffers a foreign equivalent of IHT.

- DTR is the lower of the UK IHT on the asset (at the average rate) and the foreign tax.
- The DTR is deducted from the IHT.

Location of assets

- Immovable property – where situated
- Debts – where debtor resident
- Registered shares – where registered
- Bank account – where branch situated
- Goodwill – where business carried on

Transfers between spouses/civil partners

- Both UK domiciled: Completely exempt
- To non-UK domiciled spouse/CP: Exemption **limited** to value of nil rate band

Applies for IHT only (not IT or CGT) ■━━■ **UK domicile election**

- Non-UK domiciled spouse/CP can make a UK domicile election
- Spouse exemption = unlimited
- But brings all overseas assets within scope of UK IHT

BPR applies on lifetime and death transfers. It reduces the value transferred.

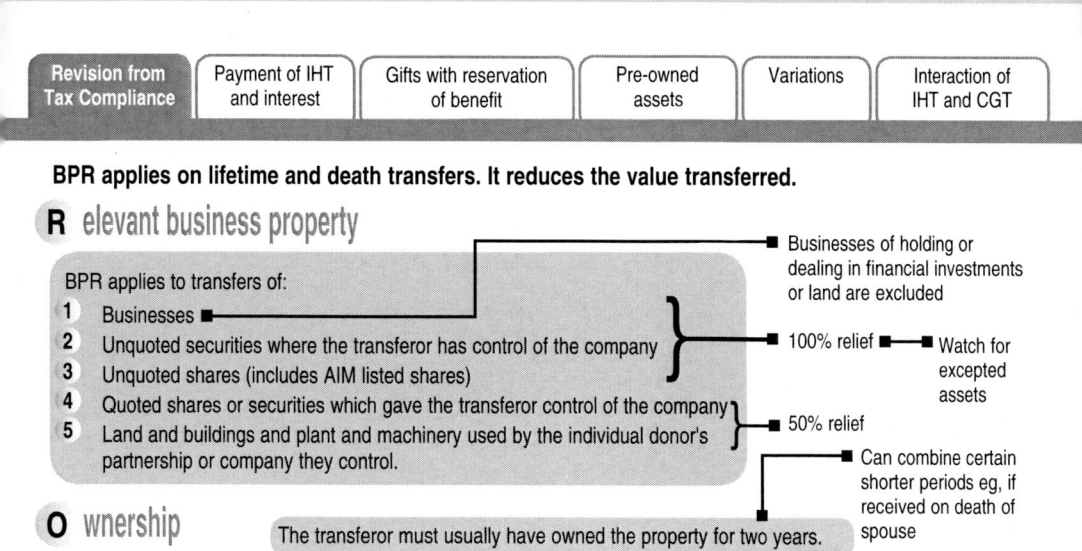

R elevant business property

BPR applies to transfers of:

1. Businesses ■
2. Unquoted securities where the transferor has control of the company
3. Unquoted shares (includes AIM listed shares)
4. Quoted shares or securities which gave the transferor control of the company
5. Land and buildings and plant and machinery used by the individual donor's partnership or company they control.

- Businesses of holding or dealing in financial investments or land are excluded
- 100% relief ■── Watch for excepted assets
- 50% relief

- Can combine certain shorter periods eg, if received on death of spouse

O wnership

The transferor must usually have owned the property for two years.

S ale contract

There must not be a binding contract for sale at date of transfer.

E xcepted assets

No relief for assets not used/needed in the business

- Exclude investment assets/surplus cash

Liabilities

Deduct liabilities relating to BPR property before deducting BPR

Withdrawal of BPR

For **lifetime transfers**, BPR does not apply when computing the tax on death if:

1. The donee has sold/gifted the property before the donor's death. ■──■ Unless full proceeds of sale used to buy qualifying replacement property

2. The donee still owns the property but is not using it for business purposes.

3. The property is no longer relevant business property.

Eg, unquoted shares have become quoted (and the donee does not control the company)

7: Inheritance tax

Instalment payments

- IHT on certain property can be paid in 10 equal annual instalments on CLTs where tax is borne by the donee, or on the death estate.
- Additionally, IHT due on PETs as a result of the death of the donor can be paid in instalments.

Land and buildings
Most unquoted shares and securities
Business/interest in business

Interest-free instalments

Not investment/property trading companies

No interest, if paid on time, on:

1. Controlling holdings in quoted shares/holdings in unquoted shares
2. BPR qualifying sole trader businesses and partnership interests

Interest-bearing instalments

Interest on outstanding balance on:

1. Non-BPR holdings in shares
2. Non-BPR qualifying sole trader businesses and partnership interests
3. Land not qualifying for BPR

Gift with reservation

A **gift with reservation** is, broadly, a gift where the donor retains some interest in the gift.

1 The gift is treated as a PET or CLT when made.

2 The gift is also either included in the death estate or treated as a PET or CLT when the reservation ceases.

The higher of the two IHT charges in (1) and (2) above is made.

The three **exceptions** to the rule are:

- When the donor gives full consideration for the reserved benefit
- When the property is land and the reservation arises because of an unforeseen change in the circumstances of the donor, being an elderly or infirm relative of the donee
- Virtual exclusion

Eg, < three lifts per month in gifted car

Pre-owned assets tax charge (POAT charge)

POAT charge aims to stop taxpayers transferring assets (usually cash) whilst still benefitting from the transferred asset

Eg, a parent gives cash to an adult child. The adult child uses the cash to purchase a house that the parent then lives in rent free.

POAT charge is an income tax charge 'Notional income' x transferor's marginal rate

- 'Notional income' is annual market rent where a house is purchased with the cash transferred
- No POAT charge if:
    - notional income does not exceed £5,000
    - transfer is to a spouse
    - cash transfer was more than seven years before the asset was first used

Variations

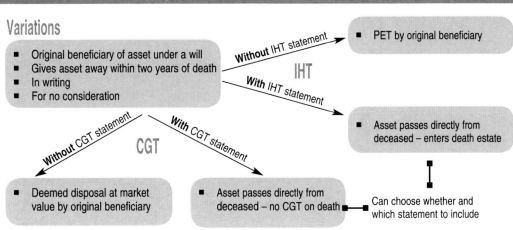

- Original beneficiary of asset under a will
- Gives asset away within two years of death
- In writing
- For no consideration

Without IHT statement → ■ PET by original beneficiary

IHT

With IHT statement → ■ Asset passes directly from deceased – enters death estate

CGT

Without CGT statement → ■ Deemed disposal at market value by original beneficiary

With CGT statement → ■ Asset passes directly from deceased – no CGT on death

Can choose whether and which statement to include

	CGT	IHT
Payable	<ul><li>Chargeable disposals by chargeable persons during lifetime</li><li>Some assets = exempt</li><li>Not payable on death (tax free uplift to MV)</li><li>Planning: transfer appreciating chargeable assets on death</li></ul>	<ul><li>Lifetime: CLTs</li><li>On death: PETs and CLTs < 7 yrs of death; all assets owned at death</li><li>No exempt assets</li><li>Some gifts are exempt eg, to spouse/ charity/political parties</li></ul>
Exempt assets	<ul><li>Cars</li><li>Cash</li><li>Chattels where original cost and consideration do not exceed £6,000</li><li>Wasting chattels unless eligible for capital allowances</li><li>Gilts, qualifying corporate bonds, national savings certificates and premium bonds, ISA investments</li></ul>	There are no exempt assets from an IHT perspective.

	CGT	IHT
Inter-spouse/CP transfers	■ No gain/no loss	■ Transfers exempt both in lifetime and on death ■ Can transfer unused nil rate band
Related property	■ No concept for CGT ■ Value assets at their stand alone value (usually MV)	■ Value assets based on ownership of donor plus holdings of related property ■ Also consider loss to donor ie, reduction in value of donor's estate as result of transfer

	CGT	IHT
Transfers that are PETs	<ul><li>If a chargeable asset = liable to CGT **unless** qualifies for gift relief</li><li>s.165 TCGA 1992 gift relief applies to business assets (s.260 cannot apply as no immediate charge to IHT on a PET)</li><li>Business asset disposal relief may be available</li></ul>	<ul><li>No IHT during lifetime</li><li>IHT may become payable if donor dies < 7 years after making gift</li><li>Taper relief if donor survives at least 3 years after making gift</li></ul>
Transfers that are CLTs	<ul><li>If a chargeable asset = liable to CGT</li><li>s.260 gift relief applies to **any** asset as also immediate charge to IHT (even if within NRB)</li><li>Business asset disposal relief may be available if gift relief not claimed</li></ul>	<ul><li>Lifetime IHT @ 20% if not covered by NRB</li><li>Further IHT may become payable if donor dies < 7 years after making gift</li><li>Taper relief is available if made at least 3 years before death</li></ul>

	CGT	IHT
Gift of shares	■ Gift relief as noted above ■ Capital gain may be eligible for Business Asset Disposal Relief (BADR) and taxed at 10%.	■ Business Property Relief (BPR) may reduce the value of the transfer by 50% or 100%. Note the requirement for shares to be retained/equivalent business property purchased for death tax on a lifetime PET.
Gift of property	■ Private residence relief may reduce gain. Be aware of any periods of absence which are not deemed occupation or any business use of property.	■ Residence Nil Rate Band (RNRB) may be available where the property was gifted on death to a direct descendant. ■ Watch out for GWROB (above).
Gift with reservation of benefit	■ If a chargeable asset = liable to CGT ■ If house gifted and not occupied by donee, no private residence relief	■ PET/CLT and also included in donor's estate ■ Choose treatment resulting in higher tax liability (usually death estate)

Notes

8: Personal tax – additional aspects

You must be able to suggest potential tax planning strategies suitable for a particular individual.

This chapter helps you to advise an individual on whether they should make a claim to use the remittance basis.

It also considers the implications of a person's residence and domicile status for a potential or past transaction.

Finally it looks at some of the different investment vehicles available to individuals looking to invest their wealth.

Domicile

- Country of permanent home
- Three main types of domicile:
  - Origin
  - Dependency
  - Choice

■ Deemed domicile applies for IT and CGT (differs to IHT definition)

Deemed domicile

Deemed domiciled for IT/CGT if:

- UK resident at least 15 of previous 20 tax years; or
- Non-domicile but
  - born in UK; and
  - UK domicile of origin; and
  - UK resident in current year.

UK resident but non-UK domiciled individuals can claim to be taxed on overseas income only when it is **remitted** to the UK.

Can only change domicile by:

- Severing ties with the old country; and
- Establishing a permanent life in the new country.

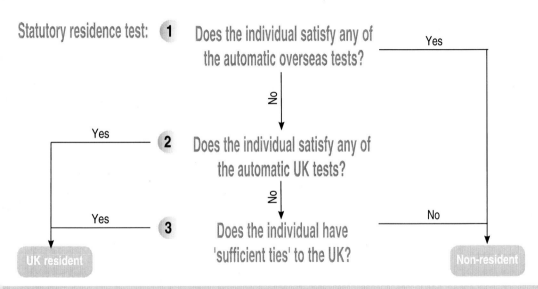

Statutory residence test:

1 Does the individual satisfy any of the automatic overseas tests? — Yes →

No ↓

2 Does the individual satisfy any of the automatic UK tests? — Yes →

No ↓

3 Does the individual have 'sufficient ties' to the UK? — Yes →

No →

UK resident

Non-resident

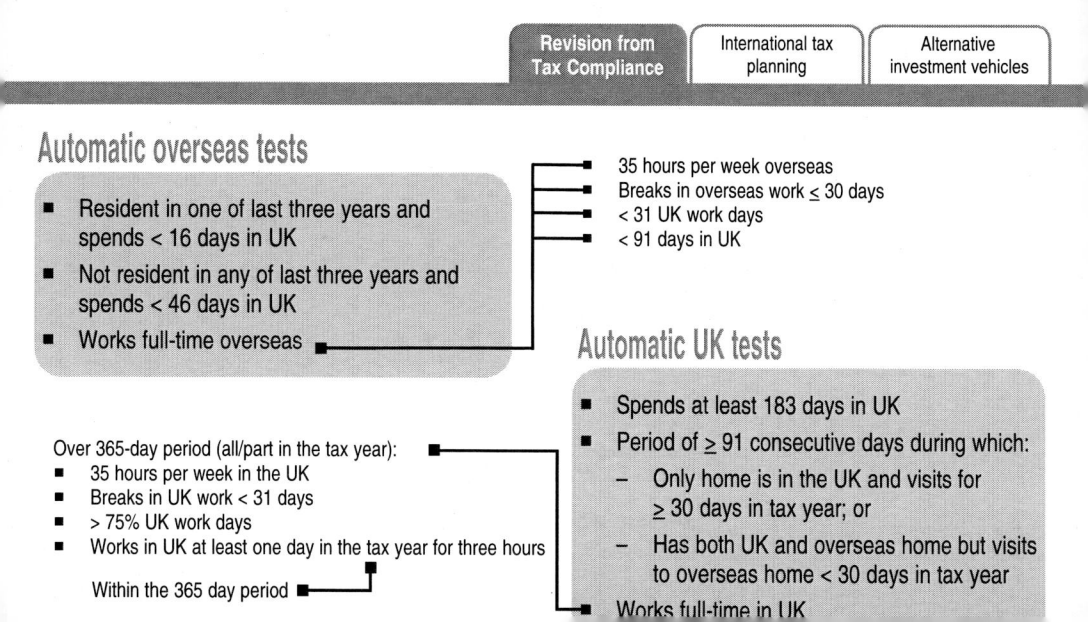

Automatic overseas tests

- Resident in one of last three years and spends < 16 days in UK
- Not resident in any of last three years and spends < 46 days in UK
- Works full-time overseas

- 35 hours per week overseas
- Breaks in overseas work ≤ 30 days
- < 31 UK work days
- < 91 days in UK

Automatic UK tests

- Spends at least 183 days in UK
- Period of ≥ 91 consecutive days during which:
  - Only home is in the UK and visits for ≥ 30 days in tax year; or
  - Has both UK and overseas home but visits to overseas home < 30 days in tax year
- Works full-time in UK

Over 365-day period (all/part in the tax year):
- 35 hours per week in the UK
- Breaks in UK work < 31 days
- > 75% UK work days
- Works in UK at least one day in the tax year for three hours

Within the 365 day period

Ties

May be able to split the tax year ▶▶ see later

- Family
- Accommodation
- Work
- 90 days
- More time in the UK than elsewhere? ■

■ Only consider final tie if was resident in at least one of the three previous tax years

Days in UK in tax year	Leavers	Arrivers
0–15	Not resident	Not resident
16–45	Resident if 4 ties	Not resident
46–90	Resident if 3 ties	Resident if 4 ties
91–120	Resident if 2 ties	Resident if 3 ties
121–182	Resident if 1 tie	Resident if 2 ties
183 or more	Resident	Resident

8: Personal tax – additional aspects

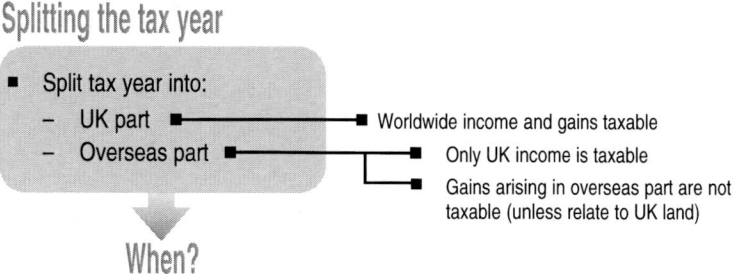

Splitting the tax year

- Split tax year into:
  - UK part ■ ——————— ■ Worldwide income and gains taxable
  - Overseas part ■
    - ■ Only UK income is taxable
    - ■ Gains arising in overseas part are not taxable (unless relate to UK land)

When?

Leavers
- They (or spouse) start full-time work overseas
  ▶ see later

Arrivers
- They (or spouse) start full-time work in the UK
- They (or spouse) return from full-time work overseas

Remittance basis

Income taxed only when brought into the UK

If individual is:
- Non-UK domiciled; and
- Has foreign income.

Foreign income taxed on arising basis unless remittance basis claimed.

Remittance basis **automatically** applies if the individual has:
- Unremitted income/gains in tax year < £2,000; or
- No UK gains and UK investment income ≤ £100 which has been taxed in the UK **and** makes no remittances in the tax year **and** either aged < 18 or been resident in UK for not more than six years out of last nine.

Applies if deemed domicile, but otherwise cannot claim RB

If remittance basis is **claimed**:
- No personal allowance
- £30,000 RBC if UK resident for ≥ 7 years out of previous 9 tax years **and** aged >18 years

RBC increases to:
- £60,000 when resident for ≥ 12 out of previous 14 tax years

TP067-305Z3-0002

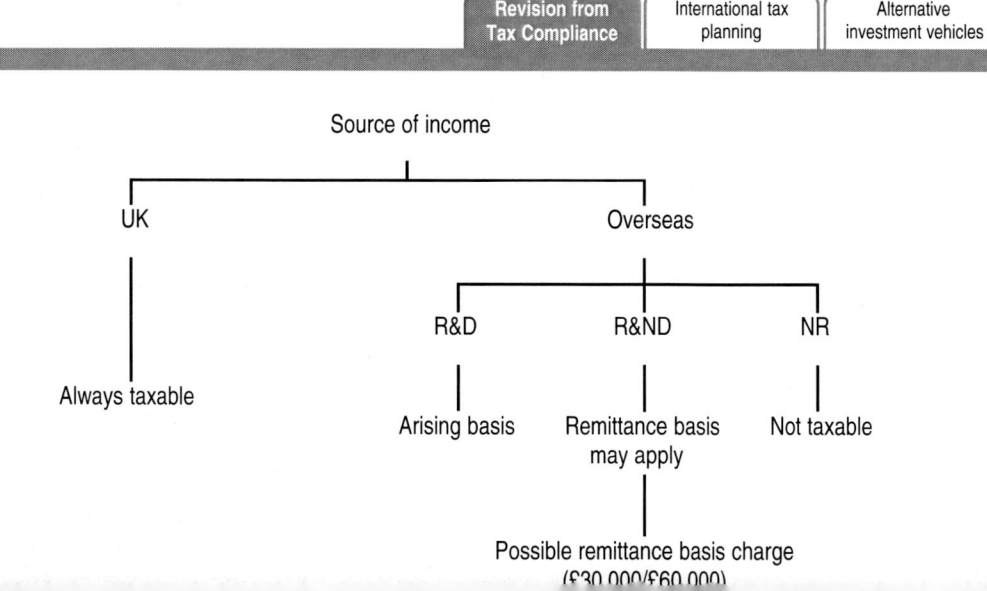

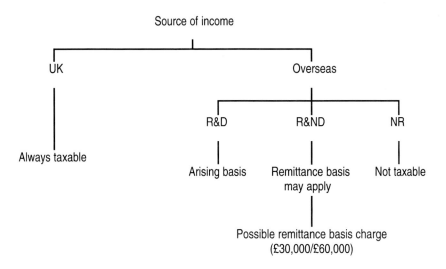

Employment income

1	Resident and domiciled in UK	Taxable on **worldwide** earnings
2	Resident but not domiciled	■ Taxable on **worldwide** earnings in UK ■ **But** may claim **remittance** basis for overseas earnings if employer non-UK resident
3	Not resident in UK	■ UK earnings taxed in UK ■ Foreign earnings **not** taxable

Other income

- **Foreign dividends** – taxed in the same way as UK dividends

- **Overseas interest** – taxed in the same way as UK savings income

- **Overseas trade** – profits calculated as for UK trade

- **Overseas rental income** – taxed in same way as UK rental income

Taxed on **arising** basis unless the **remittance** basis applies ie, if the individual is not domiciled in the UK.

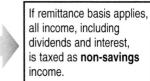

If remittance basis applies, all income, including dividends and interest, is taxed as **non-savings** income.

Double tax relief is given to prevent income being taxed in both the UK and overseas.

1 Agreements

Relief may be given under an agreement between the two countries.

If no agreement →

2 Credit relief

- Foreign income brought into the tax computation gross
- Treated as the **top slice** of individual's income
- Relief = lower of:
  - The foreign tax; and
  - The UK tax.
- Deduct from the UK tax

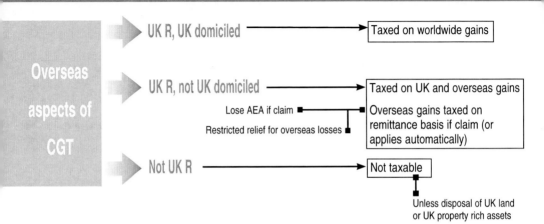

Double taxation relief (DTR)

Available if gain taxed both in UK and overseas

Calculated based on sterling figures

Relief for lower of UK and overseas tax

Deemed UK domicile – in gain calculation use MV at 5.4.17 (instead of cost) for assets held at 5.4.17

Residential property-CGT on post 5 April 2015 gain

Non-residential/property rich asset – CGT on post 5 April 2019 gain

Return/pay within 60 days

Overseas employment

If conditions satisfied, can split the tax year into UK and overseas parts if leave during the year to work full time overseas

Tax free overseas employment expenses

- Overseas board and lodgings
- Any number of visits home
- Travel costs for up to two return visits of spouse and minor children if period of absence at least 60 continuous days

Planning considerations when employed abroad

Must choose whether:

- To claim to use remittance basis and (maybe) pay RBC, lose PA and AEA
- Not claim and pay tax on all UK and overseas income as normal

- Timing – stay outside UK for required time period
- Separate income and capital funds if remittance basis applies
- Claim to receive bank interest gross NRs cannot contribute to ISAs
- Re-occupation of private residence needed to qualify for deemed occupation (unless prevented due to employment)

CGT planning

- May be able to split the tax year for CGT purposes
- Watch for temporary non-residence rules if do not remain outside the UK for five years or more ➤ see later
- Remittance basis (RB) for CGT available to non-UK domiciled individuals ━━ Exemptions available if:
- RB users must make irrevocable election in first year of using RB to be able to use **overseas losses**

    - Invest funds within 45 days of bringing them into UK
    - Bring asset to UK for sale and send proceeds overseas within 45 days

Must offset losses in set order ie, against:

1 Remitted overseas gains
2 Unremitted overseas gains

Temporary non-residence

■————————■ Cash flow advantage?

- Individual becomes non-resident;
- Was UK resident for four out of seven tax years before leaving the UK; and
- Remains non-resident for five or fewer complete years.

Income

Income remitted to the UK by non-UK domiciliary while outside the UK
■
|
■

Certain foreign income received or remitted to the UK while temporarily non-resident, is taxed on in the tax year of return to UK

Gains

- If gain/loss arises while non-resident
- On asset acquired before became non-resident
- Gain taxed/loss allowed in tax year of return to UK
■

Except UK residential property – taxed whilst non-resident

Family Investment Company (FIC)

Shareholders are family members. Usually controlled and run by the parents as directors

- Parents subscribe for voting shares to maintain control
- Non-voting shares gifted to children
  OR
- Cash gifted and children subscribe for non-voting shares
- Discretionary trust could subscribe for non-voting shares.

- Disposal for CGT (likely before significant value accrues)
- Cash is exempt from CGT
- Gift of shares/cash is a PET for IHT

  BPR unlikely as usually investment company

Taxation of the FIC

- Income subject to CT (19%) rather than IT (up to 45%)
- Likely to be a close investment holding company so will be subject to 25% CT from FY23
- Most dividends not taxable for companies
- Tax relief on interest
- Capital gains subject to CT – potential for substantial shareholding exemption to be available (see chapter 9)

Taxation of the shareholders

- IT on salary/dividends extracted – potential double taxation.
- Can manage distributions to take advantage of personal allowance and dividend allowance of adult children.

Family Investment Company (FIC) – advantages and disadvantages

Advantages	Disadvantages
Non-tax	
Parents retain control of assets	Additional costs of incorporating and running a company
Straightforward structure	Additional administration requirements
Provides asset protection	
Children can become engaged in investment planning enabling control to be gradually passed over	

Advantages	Disadvantages
Tax	
Lower corporation tax rate than income tax rate	Corporation tax rate increasing so less of a benefit especially on gains
Tax efficient extraction for young adults	Double taxation on profits extracted
More relief for interest and management expenses	Stamp duty/stamp duty land tax costs if assets are purchased/transferred from the parents
Dividends generally not taxable for companies	
Exemptions available to companies eg, SSE	
Funding through interest free loans or preference shares may be tax efficient.	

What is a trust?

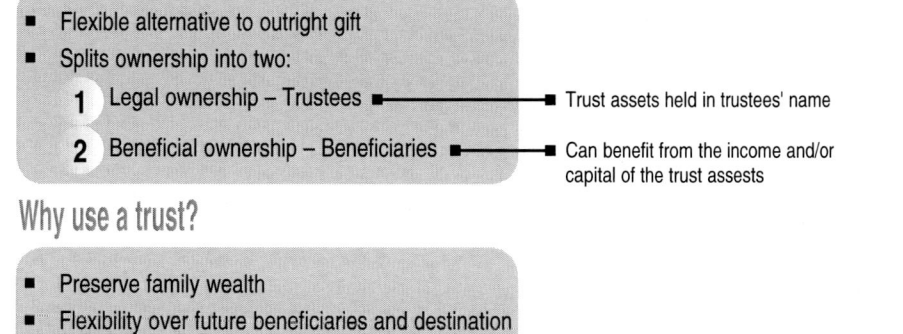

- Flexible alternative to outright gift
- Splits ownership into two:

  1 Legal ownership – Trustees — Trust assets held in trustees' name

  2 Beneficial ownership – Beneficiaries — Can benefit from the income and/or capital of the trust assests

Also called a 'settlement'

Why use a trust?

- Preserve family wealth
- Flexibility over future beneficiaries and destination of property

Types of trust

Interest in possession trust:
- Beneficiary (the '**life tenant**') has right to receive income (an '**interest in possession**')
- Capital passes to other beneficiary ('**remainderman**') when IIP comes to end

Discretionary trust:
- No beneficiary entitled to income or capital
- Up to discretion of the trustees which beneficiary benefits and how

Bare trust: Trustee is legal owner but beneficiary is absolutely entitled to property and its income

All discretionary trusts and interest in possession trusts set up during the settlor's lifetime since 22 March 2006 are **relevant property trusts (RPTs)**.

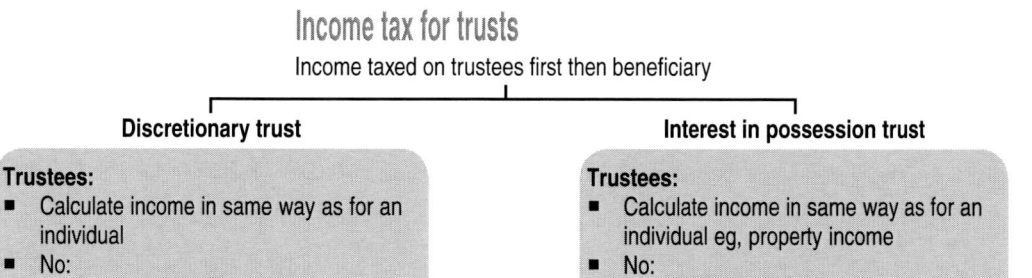

Income tax for trusts

Income taxed on trustees first then beneficiary

Discretionary trust

Trustees:
- Calculate income in same way as for an individual
- No:
  - Personal allowance
  - Savings nil rate band
  - Dividend nil rate band
  - Bands of income
- First £1,000 of income taxed at basic rate
- Rest of income taxed at trust rates:

Interest in possession trust

Trustees:
- Calculate income in same way as for an individual eg, property income
- No:
  - Personal allowance
  - Savings nil rate band
  - Dividend nil rate band
  - Bands of income
- No deduction of trust management expenses

Beneficiary:

- Taxed only when receive income payment(s)
- Payments come with 45% tax credit
- Include gross amount in tax computation
- Include always taxed as non-savings income
- Taxed at beneficiary's rate

Deemed to be paid out of the 'tax pool' of tax paid by the trustees.

- If trustees paid more tax than they needed to cover the tax credits excess is carried forward
- if trustees have not paid enough tax to cover the tax credits must pay extra tax over to HMRC.

Beneficiary:

- Entitled to trust's net income (ie, after trust management expenses)
- Income retains its nature (eg, rental income received by trust is taxed as rental income in beneficiary's hands)
- Taxed at beneficiary's rate(s)

Bare trust

- Deemed disposal by settlor at mv on assets in
- PET so gift relief only on business assets
- Disposal of assets by trust treated as being made by beneficiary – full AEA and individual rates

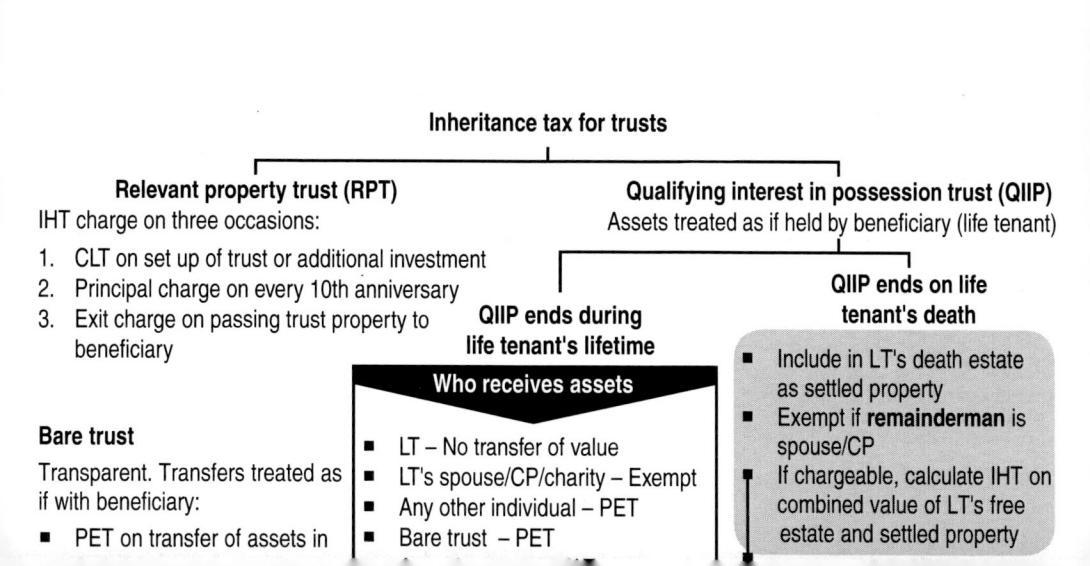

Inheritance tax for trusts

Relevant property trust (RPT)

IHT charge on three occasions:

1. CLT on set up of trust or additional investment
2. Principal charge on every 10th anniversary
3. Exit charge on passing trust property to beneficiary

Bare trust

Transparent. Transfers treated as if with beneficiary:

- PET on transfer of assets in

Qualifying interest in possession trust (QIIP)

Assets treated as if held by beneficiary (life tenant)

QIIP ends during life tenant's lifetime

Who receives assets

- LT – No transfer of value
- LT's spouse/CP/charity – Exempt
- Any other individual – PET
- Bare trust – PET

QIIP ends on life tenant's death

- Include in LT's death estate as settled property
- Exempt if **remainderman** is spouse/CP
- If chargeable, calculate IHT on combined value of LT's free estate and settled property

Capital gains tax for trusts

Gifts to trust

RPT
Deemed disposal at market value

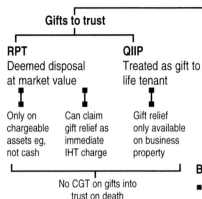

Only on chargeable assets eg, not cash

Can claim gift relief as immediate IHT charge

QIIP
Treated as gift to life tenant

Gift relief only available on business property

No CGT on gifts into trust on death

Disposals by trust

- Annual exempt amount £6,150 (2022/23)
- Split between all trusts set up by same settlor — Minimum £1,230
- CGT at 20% on most assets, 28% on residential property not qualifying for PRR

Gift relief may be claimed on disposal by RPT **only** as immediate charge to IHT (exit charge)

Bare trust

- Deemed disposal by settlor at mv on assets in
- PET so gift relief only on business assets
- Disposal of assets by trust treated as being made by beneficiary – full AEA and individual rates

Pension schemes

SSAS = special occupational scheme for small companies with relaxed borrowing and lending rules

→

May hold the company's commercial (but not usually residential) property

←

SSAS = special personal pension scheme for small companies with relaxed borrowing rules

Can borrow up to 50% fund value

Can lend up to 50% of the fund value to its own company

Can borrow up to 50% fund value

9: Corporation tax for a single company

Topic List

Corporation tax computation

R&D expenditure

IFAs

Companies with investment business

Some of the topics in this chapter eg, the corporation tax computation and administration, are revision from Tax Compliance.

You must be aware of when an additional deduction may be made for research and development expenditure and when a tax credit may be claimed.

It is essential that you can explain when the disposal of a shareholding is an exempt disposal.

Residence

A UK resident company is chargeable on its worldwide profits. A company is resident in the UK if it is incorporated in the UK or if its central management and control are in the UK.

Period of account

A period of account is the period for which accounts are prepared.

Accounting period

An accounting period is the period for which corporation tax is charged.

Alert! An accounting period can never be > 12 months.

If a company prepares accounts for a longer period, it must be split into 2 CT accounting periods.

1st 12 months form the 1st accounting period

Remaining months form the 2nd accounting period

- Begins when the company starts to trade, acquires a source of income or immediately after the end of the previous accounting period.
- Ends 12 months after it starts, when the period of account ends, when it starts or ceases to trade or when it ceases to be UK resident.

Taxable total profits

A company's **taxable total profits** are arrived at by adding together its various sources of income and chargeable gains and then deducting qualifying donations.

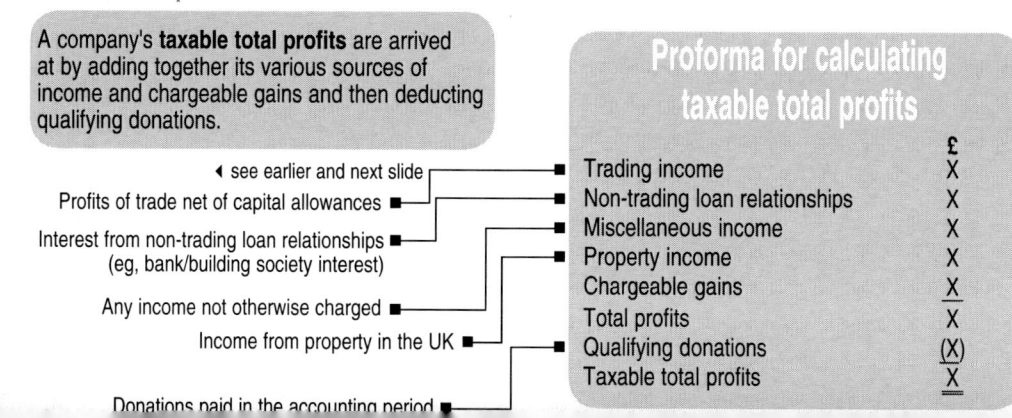

Proforma for calculating taxable total profits

	£
Trading income	X
Non-trading loan relationships	X
Miscellaneous income	X
Property income	X
Chargeable gains	X
Total profits	X
Qualifying donations	(X)
Taxable total profits	X

◀ see earlier and next slide — Trading income

Profits of trade net of capital allowances ■

Interest from non-trading loan relationships ■
(eg, bank/building society interest)

Any income not otherwise charged ■

Income from property in the UK ■

Donations paid in the accounting period ■

Capital allowances for companies

Most capital allowances rules are the same for companies and individuals.

Not available on cars or second-hand assets

Difference

No private use adjustment required for companies (private use is taxed as benefit on employee)

Temporary FYAs

Temporary FYAs of 130% on main pool assets (super-deduction) and 50% on special rate pool assets for expenditure incurred from 1 April 2021 to 31 March 2023, for companies only.

- Claim AIA on special rate assets
- Claim super-deduction on R&D main pool assets rather than 100% R&D FYA

Immediate balancing charge on disposal of assets on which the super-deduction or the special rate FYA has been claimed.

For special rate assets:
BC = 50% proceeds

For super-deduction:

BC = proceeds for disposal in AP commencing after 1 April 2023

BC = 1.3 × proceeds in AP ending prior to 1 April 2023

BC = 1.3 × proceeds proportionately reduced for APs straddling 1 April 2023

Corporation tax rate

Rate of corporation tax (CT) is set for financial years

A financial year runs from 1 April in one year to 31 March in the next. **Financial Year 2022 (FY2022) runs from 1 April 2022 to 31 March 2023.**

19% for FY22

If there is a change in the rate of CT, and a company's accounting period does not fall entirely into one Financial

Future corporation tax rates

FY23:

- 19% for small profits rate companies (augmented profits of £50,000 or less)
- 25% for main rate companies (augmented profits at least £250,000)
- Marginal relief where augmented profits are between the limits
- Limits divided by number of associated companies

Augmented profit £50,000 to £250,000
CT at 25%   X
Less marginal relief:

U = upper limit (£250,000)

A = augmented profits

Augmented profits (AP) ■──■ Taxable total profits plus exempt ■──■ UK and overseas dividends
ABGH distributions from non-51% subsidiaries

≤ £1.5 million   > £1.5 million   > £20 million

- Multiply by months/12 for short accounting periods
- Share equally between the number of 'related 51% group companies'

Payment due date is 9 months + 1 day after end of the accounting period

Payment due in instalments unless:

- CT liability < £10,000, or
- Not large in PY, and AP ≤ £10m

Starting in month 7 for > £1.5m
Starting in month 3 for > £20m

Related 51% group company

- Include 51% direct and indirect subsidiaries at the end of the previous accounting period
- Ignore passive companies

Example

A Ltd, which has one related 51% group company, prepares accounts for the nine months to 31.3.23. The limit for this period is:

$$9/12 \times \frac{1,500,000}{2}$$

$$= £562,500$$

| Corporation tax computation | R&D expenditure | IFAs | Companies with investment business | Substantial shareholding exemption |

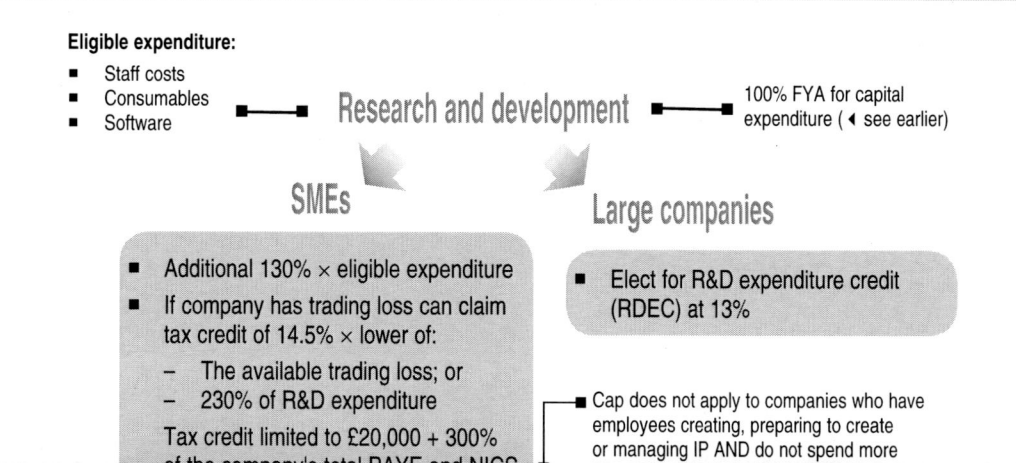

Eligible expenditure:

- Staff costs
- Consumables
- Software

Research and development

100% FYA for capital expenditure (◄ see earlier)

SMEs

- Additional 130% × eligible expenditure
- If company has trading loss can claim tax credit of 14.5% × lower of:
  - The available trading loss; or
  - 230% of R&D expenditure

  Tax credit limited to £20,000 + 300% of the company's total PAYE and NICS

Large companies

- Elect for R&D expenditure credit (RDEC) at 13%

Cap does not apply to companies who have employees creating, preparing to create or managing IP AND do not spend more than 15% of their qualifying R&D exp on

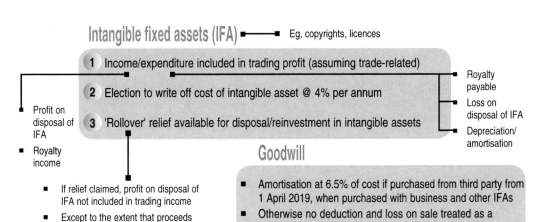

Intangible fixed assets (IFA) ■———■ Eg, copyrights, licences

1. Income/expenditure included in trading profit (assuming trade-related)

2. Election to write off cost of intangible asset @ 4% per annum

3. 'Rollover' relief available for disposal/reinvestment in intangible assets

- Royalty payable
- Loss on disposal of IFA
- Depreciation/ amortisation

- Profit on disposal of IFA
- Royalty income

- If relief claimed, profit on disposal of IFA not included in trading income
- Except to the extent that proceeds have not been reinvested in new asset

Goodwill

- Amortisation at 6.5% of cost if purchased from third party from 1 April 2019, when purchased with business and other IFAs
- Otherwise no deduction and loss on sale treated as a non-trading debit

Companies with investment business

Includes trading companies with shares in subsidiary

Management expenses

- Expenses of management are deductible in computing taxable profits
- Carry forward or group relieve unused expenses of management

Interest on loans to purchase investments are loan relationship debits not management expenses

Changes in ownership ▶▶ see Chapter 12

- New owner cannot use excess management expenses if reason for sale = to use them
- Management expenses lost if significant increase in company's capital after change

Losses on share sale

A loss on a sale of subscriber shares in a trading company by an 'investment company' can be relieved against:

Significant means post-change capital:

- Increases by £1m; and
- Is ≥ 125% of pre-change

Substantial shareholding exemption

1. Company owns 10% or more in a trading company
2. For 12 months over a 6-year period
3. Gain on sale of shares is exempt (loss is not allowable)

Share for share relief may be available

10: Raising finance

Topic List

Loan relationships

Foreign exchange

Leases

Debt vs equity

This chapter explores the more advanced aspects of raising finance including loan relationships, foreign exchange and using leases.

You need to be able to explain the impact, for both the investor and the company, of providing equity finance and/or debt finance.

Loan relationships

Subject to corporate interest restrictions ▸▸ see later ━━■ **Loan relationships** ■━━ Anti-avoidance rules for connected party loans

'Money debt' arising from the lending of money
Rules cover not just interest but expenses, and capital profits and losses on disposal

Trading loan relationship

- Held for trade purposes (eg, debentures issued to acquire plant and machinery)
- Costs (eg, interest accruing) are deductible trading expenses
- Income accruing (eg, interest income) is taxable as trading income

- Usually only banks/financial institutions receive trade related interest income
- However, Interest and FOREX movements in respect of trade debts = trading loan relationships
  ▸▸ see below

Non-trading loan relationship

- Held for non-trade purposes (eg, debentures issued to buy shares)
- Income accruing taxed as income from non-trading loan relationship
- Deduct expenses accruing from non-trading loan relationship income; a net deficit may arise

Net deficits are relieved as follows:
- Against other profits of same accounting period
- Against non-trading income from loan relationships in previous 12m
- Group relieved
- Carried forward (see Chapter 11)

Non-trading loan relationship

Debits	Credits
Interest payable	Interest receivable
Foreign exchange losses	Foreign exchange gains
Premium on a loan liability	Discount on a loan liability
Incidental costs of loan finance	
Interest on overdue corporation tax	
Impairment loss on an unpaid business payment	

Paying interest

Company pays interest net of 20% income tax unless payable:

- To another UK company;
- On listed Eurobonds or gilts;
- On 'short' loans (not > 12 months; or
- To a non-resident (under double tax treaty).

Examples:
- Bringing loan relationship into existence (including abortive costs)

FOREX gains/losses on:	Tax treatment
Settled trading transactions	Trading income/expense
Monetary items ■ Receivables ■ Payables ■ Overdrafts ■ Loans	■ Loan relationship credit/debit ■ As recorded in the accounts ■ Trading/non-trading as appropriate
Non-monetary items ■ Capital assets	Part of capital profit/loss on sale

■ Use sterling, except for ships, aircraft and shares
■ For those use tax currency and convert to sterling at date of transaction

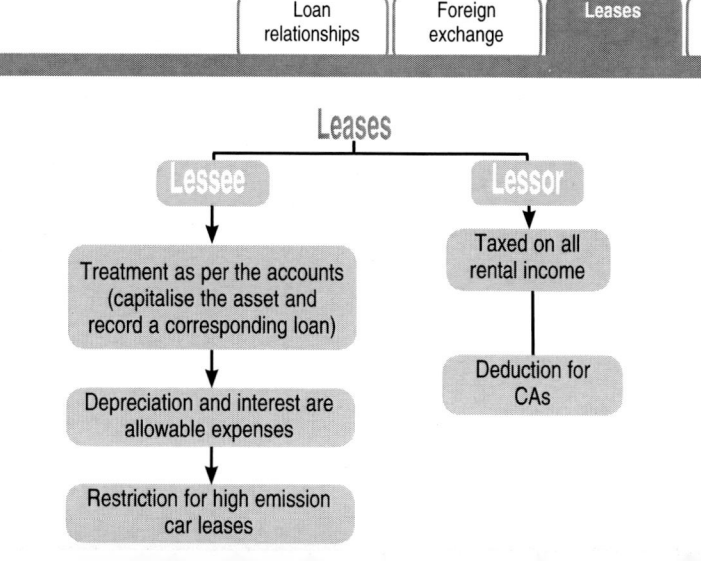

Leases

Lessee

- Treatment as per the accounts (capitalise the asset and record a corresponding loan)
- Depreciation and interest are allowable expenses
- Restriction for high emission car leases

Lessor

- Taxed on all rental income
- Deduction for CAs

Equity vs debt

	Distribution	Interest
Paying co	Not tax deductible	Tax deductible
Private investor	Taxed at 0%/8.75%/33.75%/39.35%	■ Taxable at 0%/20%/40%/45%
Corporate investor	■ Not taxable ■ May affect augmented profits ■ SSE for gain?	■ Taxable loan relationship ■ Profit/loss also taxable loan relationship

11: Corporation tax losses

Topic List

Corporate loss relief rules

Change in ownership

Choice of loss relief

This chapter begins by recapping the rules on corporation tax losses, and adding additional rules that were not tested at Tax Compliance.

You will be expected to be able to explain loss relief options for trading and non-trading losses available to a company.

You must also be able to calculate the taxable total profits after the losses are relieved and determine when

Property losses

- Automatically set off against other profits of the same AP.
- Excess losses can be:
  - Carried forward as a property loss and set off in part or in whole (by election)
  - Group relieved

Capital losses

- Can only be set against chargeable gains in current or future accounting periods
- Must be set against the first available gains
- Subject to restriction

  - Capital losses on disposal of qualifying shares by an investment company may be offset against total income for current AP and the previous 12 months.

Trading losses

A company's trading loss may be:

(1) Set against other profits of the **same** accounting period (s.37(3)(a)).

(2) Set against profits of the **previous 12 months** (s.37(3)(b)).

(3) Carried forward (see later).

Before QCDs

If pro-rating is necessary, pro-rate profits before QCDs to compute maximum relief

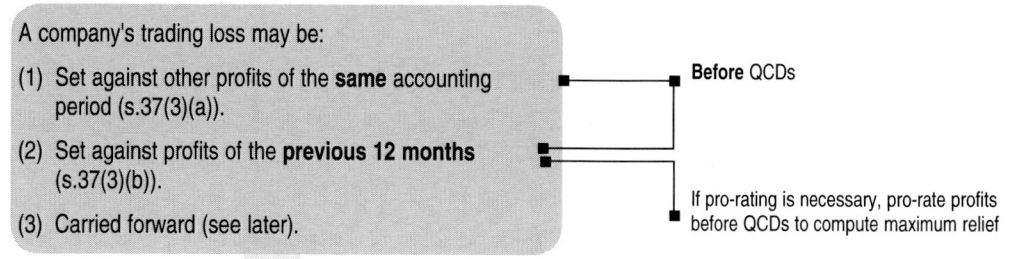

- If claiming relief (2), must claim relief (1) first.
- Both are all or nothing claims.

Terminal loss relief – last 12 months (s.37)

12 month CB period extended to 36 months where trading loss arose in 12 months before trade ceases.

Carried forward trading losses

- Usually against total profits (whole or part of loss) (s.45A)
- No claim to carry forward but claim for amount to relieve (two years of end of AP)

Terminal loss relief – carried forward losses (s.45F)

- Carry back three years from end of terminal period LIFO
- Usually against total profits
  - Not in period of loss or before period of loss

Non-trading loan relationship deficit

Set off against:

- Other profits of same AP
- Non-trading loan relationship income of previous 12 months
- Profits of group companies
- Carried forward against total profits

- Can make partial claims
- Preserves DTR credits/other CT reliefs

Restriction on carry forward relief

(offset of profits arising post-1 April 2017 and
capital gains arising post-1 April 2020)

Deductions allowance

Maximum deduction =
£5 million + 50% excess profits

- Trading losses
- NTLR deficits
- Property losses
- Management expenses
- Capital losses

Profits before deducting:

- c/f losses
- c/b reliefs
- c/f group relief (see later)

Look separately at relief against:

- Capital gains (eg, capital losses)
- Total profits

Company can choose how much of
the £5 million allowance is allocated to
each type of profit or gain

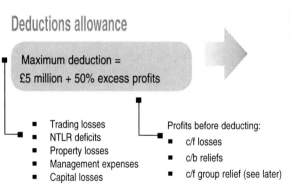

Change in ownership

1 If in any period of three years there is a change in ownership **and** a major change in nature or conduct of trade; or

2 Scale of trading becomes negligible followed by a change in ownership followed by revival of trade.

Applies if both events within:

- Five years for both changes (not starting more than three years before ownership change)

Restrictions on losses

- Trading losses cannot be carried forward past date of change in ownership
- Trading losses cannot be carried back prior to date of change in ownership
- Shell company cannot carry non-trade debits/deficits on loan relationships or IFAs forwards or back from date of change in ownership

Has no trade, investment or UK property business

The choice between reliefs

- Consider timing: earlier relief is better than later relief
- Avoid losing relief for qualifying donations
- Impact on instalment payments
- Increasing main rate of corporation tax

12: Anti-avoidance for owner-managed businesses

Topic List

Employment vs self-employment

Use of intermediaries

Close companies

Anti-avoidance legislation stops taxpayers using tax laws for unintended purposes.

You need to be able to explain why an individual might prefer to be treated as self-employed rather than employed.

In addition, you must understand when the intermediaries legislation applies and the tax implications for the company and owner.

You also need to be able to identify a close company and explain the tax implications for the company and

Use HMRC guidance to decide if an individual's income should be taxed as employment or trading income.

Employee

Contract of service

- Have to do the work themselves
- Someone can tell them what to do, and when and how to do it
- Provided with holiday pay, sick pay or a pension
- Paid hourly/weekly or given number of hours a week or month
- Work wholly or mainly for one business
- Expected to work at the premises of the person they are working for

Self employed

Contract for services

- Responsible for how the business is run
- Risk own capital
- Bear losses as well as taking profits
- Control
- Provide the major items of equipment needed to do job
- Can hire people to do the work
- Have to correct unsatisfactory work in own time and at own expense

Check Employment Status for Tax (CEST) is a useful online tool to help determine status.

Tax consequences	Employed	Self employed
Type of income	Employment income	Trading income
Basis of assessment	Receipts basis	Current year basis, with special rules in opening and closing years (actual basis for 2024/25 onwards)
Income assessed	■ Earnings from employment ■ Includes taxable benefits for private use	■ All trading profits ■ Adjust for private use
Allowable expenses	Wholly, exclusively and necessarily incurred in the performance of the duties of the employment	Wholly and exclusively incurred for the purposes of the trade
National insurance contributions	■ Class 1 primary ■ Class 1 secondary ■ Class 1A ■ Class 1B	■ Class 2 ■ Class 4
Payment of income tax	Monthly via PAYE system	■ IT and class 4 NICs – self-assessment

Small private organisation

Meets at least two of following criteria:

- Turnover not exceeding £10.2 million
- Balance sheet total (assets) not exceeding £5.1 million
- Average employees no more than 50

Intermediaries

Individual performs services or acts as an officer for a client through an intermediary (eg, a personal service company) which would be employment if performed directly

	Off payroll workers	IR35	Managed service companies
Applies to	Client = public sector or medium/large private sector	Client = small private sector	Managed service provider is involved with MSC eg, controls provision of services, takes % of income, controls payments made to worker
Employed/self-employed status	■ End client determines employment status ■ Issues status determination statement (SDS) to worker	■ Worker determines status	■ No determination of status

	Off payroll workers	**IR35**	**Managed service companies**
Liability	■ Deemed employer (often end client) adds worker to payroll ■ IT and NIC on deemed direct payment ■ No employment allowance	■ Calculated by PSC ■ IT and NIC on deemed employment payment ■ No employment allowance	■ Calculated by PSC ■ IT and NIC on any payments to worker not subject to PAYE/NIC ■ No employment allowance
Taxable income	Deemed direct payment = amount invoiced less expenses and materials	Deemed employment payment = income received from engagements less: ■ Amount paid to worker as salary ■ 5% flat rate on gross income ■ Expenses ■ Employers' NIC ■ Pension contributions	Amount of payment to worker less expenses and employers' NIC

Close companies

- UK company
- Controlled (> 50%) by five or fewer participators ━━━ ■ Include associates' interests
  (broadly shareholders) or any number of directors

1 Loans to participators

- Pay 33.75% of loan to HMRC (32.5% for loans before 1 April 2022)
- This is repaid by HMRC when the loan is repaid or written off

Also applies if loan made to:

- Trustees – if trust or beneficiary = participator or associate of participator
- LLP/partnership – if partner = participator or associate of participator

Loan repaid

Treat as repayment of new loan if:

- New loan of ≥ £5,000 is taken out within 30 days; or
- Balance before repayment ≥ £15,000 and intend to take new loan.

Loan written off

- Treated as a dividend for the individual
- Not deductible for the company

Exclusions

Loans to directors/employees ≤ £15,000 per borrower if:

- The borrower works full-time for the company; and
- Does not have a material interest (> 5%) in the company.

2 Benefits given to participators

- If the participator is not an employee, treat the value of benefit (calculated as for earnings) as though it were a distribution
- Disallow the actual cost in computing the company's trading profit

33.75% tax charge if:

- Part of tax avoidance arrangement; and
- No charge would otherwise arise.

Qualifying interest

- Interest on loan to purchase shares in close company is deductible
- Subject to cap on income tax reliefs ◄ see earlier

13: Groups and consortia

Topic List

You must be able to identify the companies to which a loss may be surrendered within a group and how much may be surrendered.

In addition, you must be able to determine the optimum loss relief to achieve the group's objectives.

You must also be able to identify a gains group and advise on the ways of reducing chargeable gains within that group.

Group relief group

One company must have a 75% effective interest in the other, or there must be a third company which has a 75% effective interest in both.

> Of share capital **and** income **and** net assets on a winding up

Group relief

> Restrictions if change in ownership of company

- Current period losses of one group company can be set against total profits of another.

- Carried forward losses can be set against total profits of another company.

> £5m deduction allowance applies to the group as a whole

> Co cannot claim c/f GR if it has unused c/f losses of own, and co cannot surrender c/f losses for GR if it could use them itself

Current year losses available to surrender

- Trading losses
- Excess property business losses
- Excess qualifying charitable donations (QCDs)
- Deficits on non-trading loan relationships
- Excess management expenses

Note: Different rules for capital losses ▶▶ see later

Carried forward losses available to surrender

- Trading losses available against total profits
- Non-trading loan relationship deficits
- Property business losses
- Management expenses of an investment business

Claimant company profits

Total profits available to absorb group relief are total profits after deducting:

- QCDs; and
- Current and brought forward losses.

Claim relief within two years of end of AP of loss

- Group relief claim is normally made on the claimant company's tax return.
- Notice of consent must also be given by surrendering company.

Overseas aspects of group relief

- Group relief for overseas PE's losses if:
  - Not relievable overseas
  - No PE exemption election made
  - Not carrying out separate wholly overseas trade
- Non-UK resident company trading through UK PE or with UK land gains or with UK property business, can

Overlapping accounting periods

- Strictly a current period relief.
- If APs do not coincide, profits and losses must be time-apportioned.
- Only profits and losses of period of overlap

Group payments arrangements

- Nominated group company pays instalments for all group companies.

- Can include non-instalment paying companies.

Group tax surrenders also possible

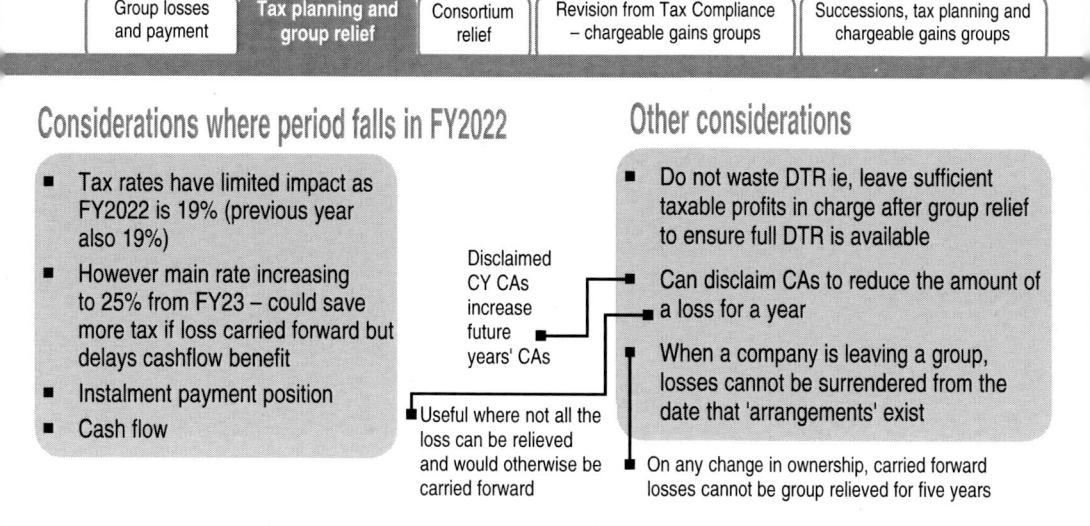

| Group losses and payment | Tax planning and group relief | Consortium relief | Revision from Tax Compliance – chargeable gains groups | Successions, tax planning and chargeable gains groups |

Considerations where period falls in FY2022

- Tax rates have limited impact as FY2022 is 19% (previous year also 19%)
- However main rate increasing to 25% from FY23 – could save more tax if loss carried forward but delays cashflow benefit
- Instalment payment position
- Cash flow

Other considerations

- Do not waste DTR ie, leave sufficient taxable profits in charge after group relief to ensure full DTR is available
- Can disclaim CAs to reduce the amount of a loss for a year
- When a company is leaving a group, losses cannot be surrendered from the date that 'arrangements' exist
- On any change in ownership, carried forward losses cannot be group relieved for five years

Disclaimed CY CAs increase future years' CAs

Useful where not all the loss can be relieved and would otherwise be carried forward

Consortia

1 If a company is 75% owned by 20 or fewer other companies, each owning at least 5%, losses can be surrendered by that company to the consortium members or vice versa.

2 Maximum surrender to/from any one member limited to:

Member's % stake $\times \dfrac{\text{consortium owned co's}}{\text{profit or loss}}$

Chargeable gains group

- Starts with principal company (must be included).
- Carries on down with 75% ordinary shareholding at each level.
- Effective interest of principal company in subsidiary company > 50%.

- Ignore actual proceeds.
- Deemed proceeds are:
  - Original cost; plus
  - Indexation to date of transfer (or up to Dec 2017 if earlier).
- Deemed proceeds become base cost for transferee company.

Intra-group transfers

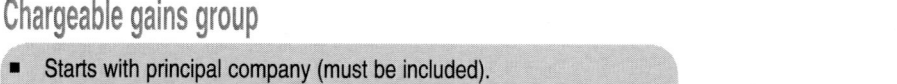

No gain/loss arises when asset is transferred within a chargeable gains group.

Degrouping charge

- Transferee leaves group within six years
- Gain at transfer added to proceeds on sale of shares

Exempt if substantial shareholding exemption available

- Unless leaving other than as a result of share sale, then gain is chargeable on the leaving company (eg, shares issued to third party)

Election

Can elect to transfer whole/part of chargeable gain/allowable loss to another member

Pre-entry capital losses

- Company with capital losses joins a group
- Use of the capital losses is restricted

- Assets sold before joining
- Assets owned when joined
- Assets acquired for business purposes from non-group companies

SSE for groups

- Investee company must be trading/part of trading group.
- Exemption does not apply to intra-group transfers.
- Can combine group shareholdings.

■ Ownership period of shares acquired via intra-group transfer = total time owned by group

Transfer of fixed assets to/from trading stock

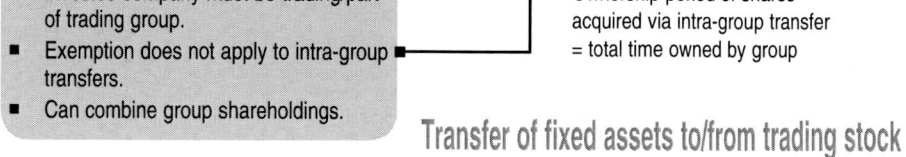

Recipient company can elect for the whole gain to be assessed as trading income on sale of stock.

- Transfer of fixed asset by one group company to another which transfers it to stock:
  - Immediate chargeable gain/allowable loss in recipient company using MV at date of transfer to stock
  - Subsequent increase in value taxed as trading income when stock sold
- Transfer of stock by one group company to another which transfers

Rollover relief

Members of a gains group may be treated as a single unit for rollover relief purposes.

Planning

Minimise group tax payable by transferring gain to company with capital losses.

    — Subject to restriction against gains incurred on or after 1 April 2020.

Succession to trade

Not a cessation if trade transferred to company with substantially the same 75% ownership

Tax consequences

- AP ends
- Predecessor can claim CAs
- Successor takes over TWDV
- Successor can use CF losses

    — Losses may be restricted by excess of relevant liabilities over relevant assets

14: International expansion

You must be able to identify whether a company is UK resident and advise on, and calculate, the UK taxation liabilities of non-UK resident companies.

Advising companies on the implications of migrating overseas is key, along with the alternative methods of establishing a business overseas.

You must be able to calculate DTR and advise on how losses and qualifying charitable donations should be used where DTR is available within a group.

Residence

A company is resident in the UK if it is:
(1) Incorporated in the UK; or
(2) Its central management and control are in the UK.

A UK resident company is subject to corporation tax on its **worldwide** profits.

Non-UK resident

A non-UK resident company is subject to corporation tax only if:

- Trades through UK **permanent establishment** (PE)
- Has profits of dealing in/developing **or investing in** land **or property** in the UK
- Has gains on UK land/ UK property rich assets

Chargeable gains

If company trades through (PE), gains on disposals of **UK assets** = taxable in UK

Held by PE or used in trade

Eg, branch, office, factory, agent

Immediate charge if:

- Non-UK company ceases trading through the UK PE
- Non-UK company exports chargeable asset

Gains on UK land/ UK property rich assets

UK residential property
CT on gains post-5 April 2015 (using MV at 5/4/2015)

UK non-residential property/ UK property rich assets
CT on gains post-5 April 2019 (using MV at 5/4/2019)

Shares with 75% of assets being UK land (at least 25% holding)

Can elect to calculate the gain based on original cost (in both cases).

Or, for residential only, can elect to use original cost and then time apportion to get post 5 April 2015 part.

Migrating from the UK

- Hard for UK incorporated company to cease being UK resident ■——■ Arrange matters so treated as resident in another territory and NR in UK under double tax treaty
- If UK resident due to management and control (M&C) in the UK, can move M&C to another country

■——■ CT accounting period ends at the date of migration

Gains on migration   ■ 'Exit charge'

- Deemed **disposal at MV** of assets if ceases to be UK resident
- Unless:
  - Asset in UK; and
  - Used in UK PE.

■ Gain on these UK assets if:
- Sold
- PE trade ceases
- Assets leave UK

Choice of overseas entity

	Overseas PE	**Overseas subsidiary**
Legal status	Single entity (ie, part of UK co)	Separate legal entity
Additional related 51% group company?	No	Yes
Income taxed in the UK company	■ PE's profits = part of trading profits ■ Unless make exemption election	Dividends not usually taxable
Basis of assessment	Arising (accruals) basis	Remittance basis (if divs taxable)
Profits taxed overseas	Yes – DTR available in UK	Yes – DTR available in UK
Overseas trading losses	■ Set against UK co's profits (unless makes exemption election) ■ If separate wholly overseas trade, only set against PE's future trade profits	■ Cannot surrender overseas loss to UK co
UK CAs	Available unless exemption election made	Not available
Transfer of assets to the	■ No gains/losses	■ Gain/losses

Incorporating an overseas PE

Implications

- PE ceases to trade (when net assets transferred to new overseas company)
- Balancing adjustments on PE assets transferred (in hands of UK company)
- Chargeable gains and losses (in UK company) on disposal of PE assets to overseas

Incorporation relief for gains

Gains can be postponed if:
- All PE assets (except cash) are transferred to the overseas company
- Consideration is wholly/mainly shares (full postponement if all consideration is shares)
- The UK company owns at least 25% of the new overseas company
- A claim is made

Gains crystallise if:

- An asset is sold within six years of transfer
  (Gain = remaining deferred gain × Gain on this asset on inc/Gross gains on inc)
- The shares in the overseas company are sold

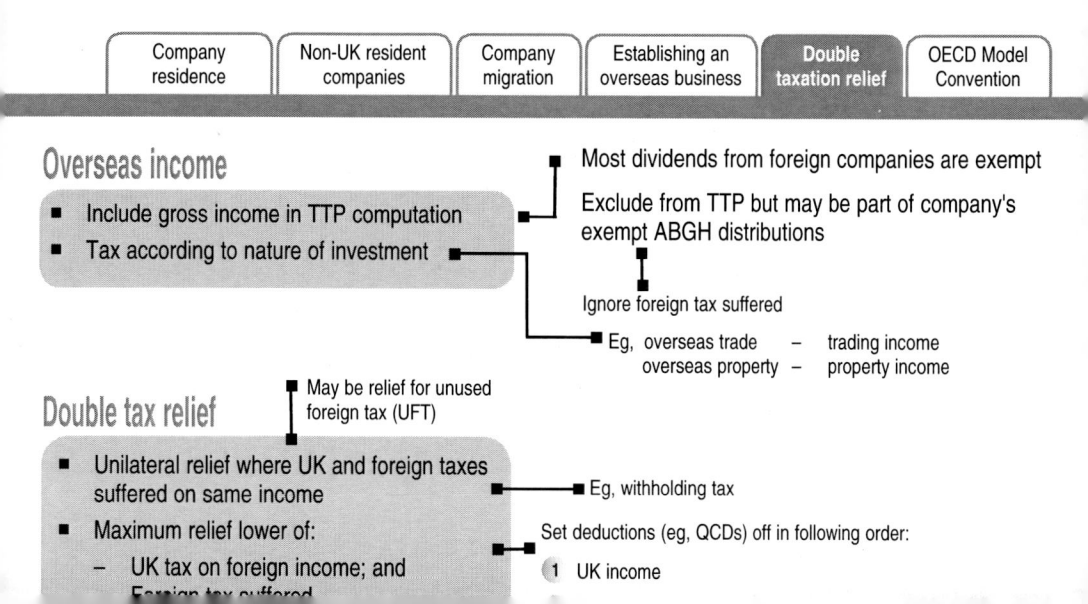

Overseas income

- Include gross income in TTP computation
- Tax according to nature of investment

- Most dividends from foreign companies are exempt

  Exclude from TTP but may be part of company's exempt ABGH distributions

  Ignore foreign tax suffered

- Eg, overseas trade   – trading income
  overseas property – property income

Double tax relief

- May be relief for unused foreign tax (UFT)

- Unilateral relief where UK and foreign taxes suffered on same income
- Maximum relief lower of:
  - UK tax on foreign income; and
  - Foreign tax suffered

- Eg, withholding tax

Set deductions (eg, QCDs) off in following order:

1   UK income

OECD model convention

Residence

Resident if liable to tax by reason of its place of management or any other criterion of similar nature

- Tie breaker clause – effective management & control

DTR

Treaty exemption;
or
Credit relief

Business profits of NR company

Only taxed in UK if UK PE

Max w'holding tax:

- Divis $\geq$ 25% = 5%
- Divis < 25% = 15%
- Interest = 10%

Permanent establishment

Fixed place of business through which business of an enterprise is carried on

Includes:	Does not include:
■ Branch ■ Office ■ Factory ■ Workshop	■ Storage facilities ■ Premises solely for purchasing etc ■ Broker or agent

15: Corporate anti-avoidance

Topic List

Value shifting

Controlled foreign companies (CFCs)

Transfer pricing

Thin capitalisation

Diverted profits tax and hybrid mismatch

You must be able to identify and explain the tax implications arising in connection with:

- *Transactions that fall within the value shifting and depreciatory transaction provisions*

- *CFC companies and the CFC charge*

- *Transfer pricing and thin capitalisation rules*

- *The diverted profits tax rules*

- *The corporate interest restriction rules*

Pre-sale dividends ■—■ 'Dividend stripping'

Cannot use to convert chargeable gains into exempt income

Depreciatory transactions

Capital loss must be reduced to level of true commercial loss

Consideration increased by 'just and reasonable' amount ■

Adjustment

Required

- Arrangements materially reduce value (ie, 'shift value' out) of shares before disposal
- Obtaining tax advantage = main purpose
- Making exempt distribution is not only part of ■—■ Eg, also involves transaction — loan financing

Not required

- No other associated transaction
- SSE applies

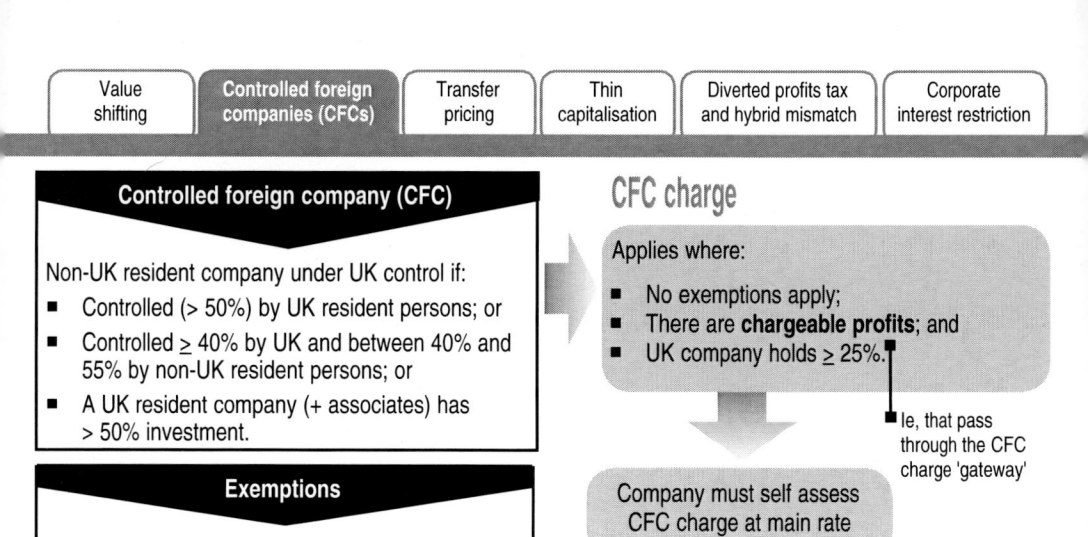

| Value shifting | **Controlled foreign companies (CFCs)** | Transfer pricing | Thin capitalisation | Diverted profits tax and hybrid mismatch | Corporate interest restriction |

Controlled foreign company (CFC)

Non-UK resident company under UK control if:

- Controlled (> 50%) by UK resident persons; or
- Controlled ≥ 40% by UK and between 40% and 55% by non-UK resident persons; or
- A UK resident company (+ associates) has > 50% investment.

Exemptions

- Exempt period
- Excluded territories
- Low profits exemption

CFC charge

Applies where:

- No exemptions apply;
- There are **chargeable profits**; and
- UK company holds ≥ 25%.

    Ie, that pass through the CFC charge 'gateway'

Company must self assess CFC charge at main rate

    May be reduced by creditable tax but not by UK losses or surplus expenses

CFC charge gateway

- Profits attributable to UK activities

Profits attributable to UK activities

If any of the following conditions are met, **no** profits pass through gateway:

- No tax planning
- No UK management
- Could manage own business if UK management stopped

If none of the conditions are met, analyse 'Significant People Functions' (SPFs)

Chargeable profits

Derived from:
- SPFs carried out in UK
- Capital investment from UK

- Carried out in UK
- By connected person

- Profits relating to SPFs pass through gateway
- Become **chargeable profits**

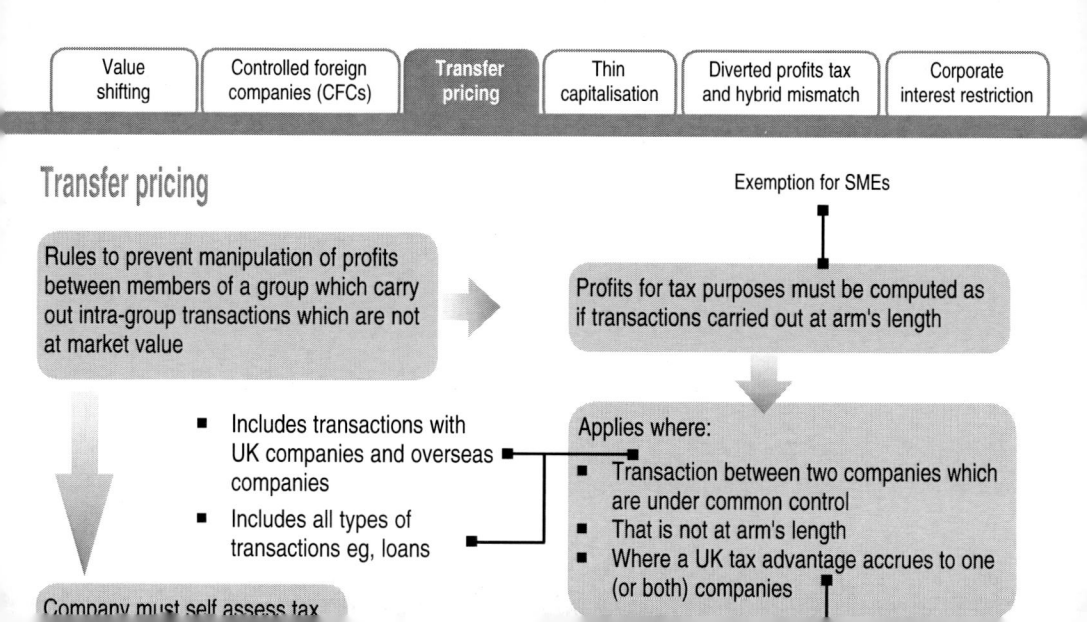

| Value shifting | Controlled foreign companies (CFCs) | **Transfer pricing** | Thin capitalisation | Diverted profits tax and hybrid mismatch | Corporate interest restriction |

Transfer pricing

Exemption for SMEs

Rules to prevent manipulation of profits between members of a group which carry out intra-group transactions which are not at market value

Profits for tax purposes must be computed as if transactions carried out at arm's length

- Includes transactions with UK companies and overseas companies
- Includes all types of transactions eg, loans

Applies where:

- Transaction between two companies which are under common control
- That is not at arm's length
- Where a UK tax advantage accrues to one (or both) companies

Company must self assess tax

Thin capitalisation

Rules apply where connected company provides loan finance at higher level of debt than a commercial bank would be prepared to lend

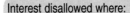

Interest disallowed where:
- Excessive loan
- Excessive rate of interest

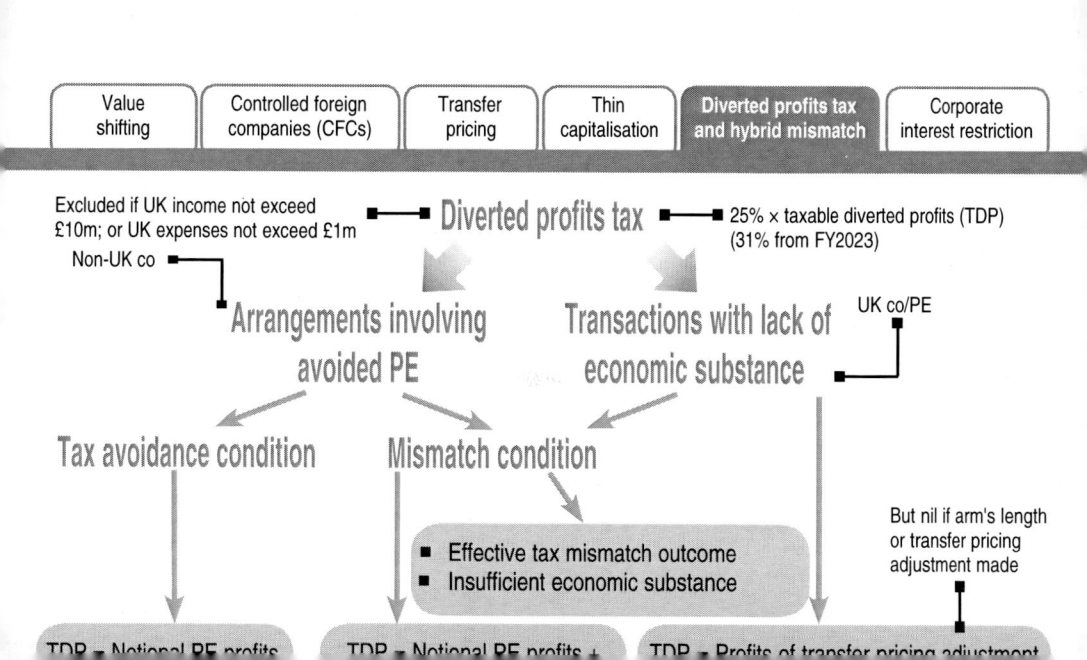

Excluded if UK income not exceed £10m; or UK expenses not exceed £1m

Non-UK co

Diverted profits tax

25% × taxable diverted profits (TDP) (31% from FY2023)

UK co/PE

Arrangements involving avoided PE

Transactions with lack of economic substance

Tax avoidance condition

Mismatch condition

- Effective tax mismatch outcome
- Insufficient economic substance

But nil if arm's length or transfer pricing adjustment made

TDP = Notional PE profits

TDP = Notional PE profits +

TDP = Profits of transfer pricing adjustment

Hybrid mismatch rules

Deny:

- Multiple deduction for same expense
- Deduction to payee without taxation of payee

Examples

- **Financial instruments** allowing deduction of payment as interest but payee treats as exempt dividend
- **Dual residence companies** obtaining expense deduction in both countries
- **PEs** recognised in only one country

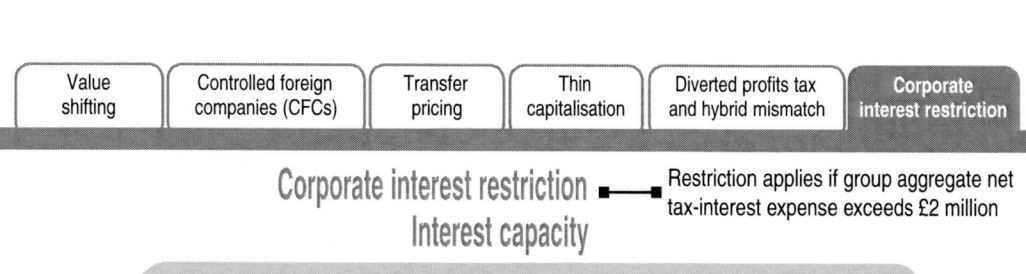

| Value shifting | Controlled foreign companies (CFCs) | Transfer pricing | Thin capitalisation | Diverted profits tax and hybrid mismatch | Corporate interest restriction |

Corporate interest restriction ━━━ Restriction applies if group aggregate net tax-interest expense exceeds £2 million
Interest capacity

- Current accounting period interest allowance, plus
- Brought forward unused interest allowance (available for five years)
- Two methods for calculating interest allowance

Fixed ratio method (Default)

Lower of
- 30% of aggregate tax – EBITDA of group
- 'fixed ratio debt cap'

Group ratio method (by election)

Lower of
- 'group ratio %' of aggregate tax-EBITDA of group
- 'group ratio debt cap'

EBITDA

Group ratio %
Net group interest expense/

Group ratio debt cap

16: Companies – special situations

Topic List

Company purchase of own shares

Tax implications of administration or liquidation

Tax planning when winding up a company

You must be able to advise on the correct treatment, and calculate the tax liabilities arising as a result, of a company purchase of its own shares from the shareholders.

You must also be able to give appropriate advice, and calculate the tax liabilities arising, in connection with a liquidation or winding up of a company.

Purchase of own shares

Individual shareholders

Treated as a capital receipt rather than a distribution (ie, dividend) if **all** of the following conditions are satisfied:

1 Purchase = for benefit of the trade

2 Vendor's stake falls to:
   - ≤ 30%, and
   - ≤ 75% of percentage holding before the purchase

3 Vendor/spouse had owned shares for ≥ five years

4 Vendor = UK R at date of repurchase

- If conditions not satisfied
  purchase = income distribution (ie, dividend)

Corporate shareholders

- Always a capital receipt
- Chargeable gain/allowable loss
- Unless SSE applies

- Capital treatment also applies if:
  - Proceeds used to pay IHT liability

Tax implications of administration

New accounting period begins when the company:

- Goes into administration
- Reaches its normal accounting date
- Ceases to be in administration
- Moves out of liquidation into administration (overrides rules on winding up)

- No other CT consequences

Tax implications of liquidation

From the date winding up begins:

- Liquidator pays all CT liabilities arising
- No restriction on c/f capital losses on insolvent liquidation
- AP ends on anniversary of winding up beginning
- Liquidator = beneficial owner of assets

Tax planning on winding up

Losses

- Cannot CF trading losses so set CY losses against total profits
- Redundancy costs increase CY loss
- Terminal loss relief available
- Terminal loss relief may be available for some c/f losses
- Only losses to date winding up started can be group relieved

Groups

Liquidation of holding co

- Group relief not available
- Gains group continues

Liquidation of subsidiary

- In group relief and gains group until final dissolution

Distribution of assets

For solvent liquidations

- Pre-commencement distributions = dividends
- Post-commencement distributions = capital

Part disposal by shareholder

Striking off:

Capital treatment only if distribution < £25,000

17: VAT

Topic List

Revision from Tax Compliance

Transfer of a going concern (TOGC)

Overseas aspects of VAT

You must be able to advise on:

- *The correct treatment of and calculate the tax liabilities arising as a result of the acquisition, intra-group transfer, or disposal of property*

- *The application of the transfer of a going concern rules*

- *The interaction of the transfer of a going concern, option to tax and capital goods scheme rules*

1 Zero rated supplies

Taxable at 0%

Eg, food, books and newspapers

2 Exempt supplies

Not taxable

Eg, insurance, education and health services

3 Standard rated supplies

Taxable at 20%

All supplies which are not zero rated, reduced rate or exempt

4 Reduced rate supplies

Taxable at 5%

Eg, fuel for domestic use, energy saving materials for homeowners, smoking cessation products and contraceptives

Alert! A person making only exempt supplies cannot recover VAT on inputs.
Contrast this with a person making zero rated (taxable supplies) who can recover VAT on inputs.

Land and buildings

1 Land – exempt

2 **New** residential dwellings – zero rated

3 Non-residential converted to residential – zero rated

4 Freehold **new** commercial buildings – standard rated ■━━━━━━━━━━━━━━■ Less than three years old

5 Other sales, leases – exempt

■ Subject to landlord's **option to tax** (not residential property)

➡

Option to tax
Advantage
☑ VAT-registered landlords can reclaim input VAT
Disadvantages
☒ Must charge VAT on rent

Capital goods scheme

Initial recovery of input tax on **certain capital goods** is adjusted to reflect variations in the taxable use of those goods.

Applies to:

- **Land and buildings** costing £250,000 or more – adjusted over 10 years
- **Computers** costing £50,000 or more – adjusted over five years
- **Boats or aircraft** costing £50,000 or more – adjusted over five years

Adjustment each year:

- Difference between taxable use percentage for first year and taxable use percentage for current year
- × 1/10 (land) or 1/5 (computers, boats and aircraft)

On sale:

- Normal annual adjustment, **plus**
- Further adjustment for remaining years assuming taxable use of 0% (exempt sale) or 100% (taxable sale)

Group registration

- Available to companies under **common control**, or where a UK individual/partnership controls a company

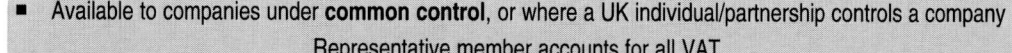

Representative member accounts for all VAT.

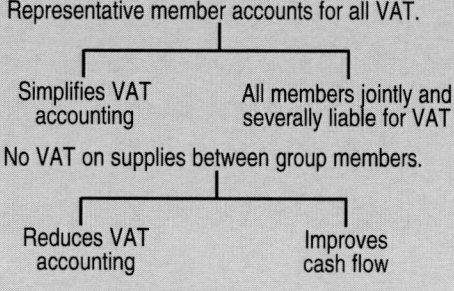

Simplifies VAT accounting

All members jointly and severally liable for VAT

No VAT on supplies between group members.

Reduces VAT accounting

Improves cash flow

- Companies only included in group if specific application made – not automatic
- Consider excluding companies making largely zero rated supplies which could claim monthly VAT

Transfer of a going concern

On a transfer of a whole business (or part that can be run on its own) there is no supply.

Excludes 'taxable land' **unless** transferee opts to tax

Conditions

- The assets must be used by the transferee in carrying on the same kind of business.
- If transferor is registered the transferee must be registered/become liable to be registered following the transfer.
- If only part transferred it must be capable of 'separate operation'.
- There must not be a 'significant' break in trading.

SI 1995/1268

Effect

1 Non-supply

- Transferor must not charge output VAT.
- If output VAT is charged, transferee cannot reclaim as input VAT.
- Any input VAT incurred by the transferor is not directly attributable to a supply for partial exemption purposes.

2 If transferor is registered, transferee must include transferor's past turnover in determining if they are liable to register.

3 Can transfer VAT registration number to new owner. If so, transfers liability for past errors.

Goods between GB & overseas (EU and non-EU)

Exports
Exports of goods to overseas are zero rated.

Imports
Imports of goods from overseas are subject to VAT at the same rate as on a sale within the UK

- Postponed VAT accounting is available to VAT registered traders to allow VAT to be paid and reclaimed on the same VAT invoice (VAT neutral if 100% taxable)

NI protocol for goods

- Supplies of goods from GB to NI are treated as exports from GB and imports into NI
- Supplies of goods from NI to GB are treated as exports from NI and imports into GB

  - UK includes both Great Britain (GB) and Northern Ireland (NI)

Supply of services

Takes place where:
- Supplier is, if customer not a relevant business person (B2C)
- Customer is, if customer is a relevant business person (B2B)

18: Stamp taxes

Topic List

Stamp duty

Stamp duty reserve tax

Stamp duty land tax

Stamp duty on incorporation or liquidation

This chapter revises the scope of the different stamp taxes that you saw in the Tax Compliance exam and covers the calculation of the relevant charges and the available exemptions.

You must now also be aware of the stamp duty impact on a corporate transformation, such as incorporation or liquidation.

Stamp duty

Paid by transferee on transfers of shares by physical **document**.

- Also known as an 'Instrument'

1 0.5% × consideration (only if > £1,000)

2 Round up to nearest £5

On MV if securities to a connected company

Stamp duty exemptions

- No chargeable consideration eg, gifts
- On divorce
- Received via someone's will on death
- Certain intra-group share transfers
- Recognised growth market securities (eg, AIM)

Administration of stamp duty

- Send document and stamp duty due to HMRC within 30 days of execution
- Late payment interest runs from end of 30-day period
- Penalty for late document:
  - ≤ 12m late: 10% of duty, capped at £300
  - 12–24m late: 20% of duty
  - > 24m late: 30% of duty
- No penalty charged if < £20

- Round down to nearest £5
- Only charged if > £25
- Will be higher if deliberate failure

Stamp duty reserve tax

No charge if no consideration (unless transfer of listed securities to connected company – then use MV)

Paid on transfers of shares not caught by stamp duty
ie, paperless transactions

1   0.5% × consideration

2   Do not round

SDRT exemptions

- No chargeable consideration eg, gifts
- On divorce
- Received via someone's will on death
- Certain intra-group share transfers
- Recognised growth market securities (eg, AIM)

Administration of SDRT

- Collected automatically via stockbrokers
- Due on:
  - 7th day of month following month of contract
  - 14 calendar days after trade date if can be made by CREST

Stamp duty land tax

Payable by purchaser on land transactions eg,
transfer of freehold land

Additional 3% if cost > £40,000 and already owns residential property (unless replacement main residence) or is a company
Additional 2% if purchaser is non-resident for purchase after 1 April 2021

First time buyers no SDLT on first £300,000 if cost does not exceed £500,000 (balance at 5%)

Companies purchasing residential property over £500,000 pay

ATED ▸▸ see later

15% rate for companies purchasing residential property valued at > £500,000

Rate (%)	Residential	Rate (%)	Non-residential
0	£Nil–£125,000	0	£Nil–£150,000
2	£125,001–£250,000	2	£150,001–£250,000
5	£250,001–£925,000	5	£250,001–and over
10	£925,001–£1,500,000		
12	£1,500,001 and over		

Temporary rates apply 8 July 2020 – 30 September 2021 (see tax tables)

Payable on amount that falls in each bracket

SDLT exemptions

- No chargeable consideration eg, gifts
- On divorce
- Received via someone's will on death
- Transfer of land between members of 75% group

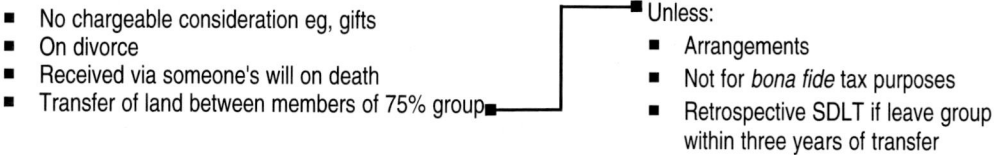

- Unless:
  - Arrangements
  - Not for *bona fide* tax purposes
  - Retrospective SDLT if leave group within three years of transfer

SDLT administration

- File land transaction return (even if no SDLT payable)
- Within 14 days of transaction
- Also pay tax within 14 days of transaction
- Late payment interest from end of 14 day period to day before SDLT paid
- Penalties for late filing:
  - Up to three months late: £100 automatic penalty
  - Over three months late: £200 automatic penalty

Company transformations

- **Incorporation**   ▶▶ see Chapter 22

  - SDLT payable on total value of all land transferred
  - If TOGC, calculate on VAT-exclusive value only
  - No SD on shares received by sole trader as new issue

- **Liquidation**   ▶▶ see Chapter 16

  - Exempt from SDLT if transferred to shareholder
  - Unless consideration given

| Stamp duty | Stamp duty reserve tax | Stamp duty land tax | Stamp duty on incorporation or liquidation | **High value properties** |

Annual tax on enveloped dwellings (ATED)

Annual tax on corporate owners of residential dwellings worth > £500,000

Reliefs

- Properties part of a property rental business
- Property developers and traders
- Certain unoccupied properties

Administration

- Return and payment within 30 days of start of FY/purchase
- Penalties for errors in return, late returns and late ATED payment

Use relief declaration return if relief available

19: Choice of business structure

Topic List

Choice of trading entity

Withdrawing profits from the business

Corporate structure

You need to be able to advise on the most appropriate business or corporate structure for a given scenario.

You must also be able to advise on the most tax efficient method of withdrawing profits from a business for a given scenario.

Sole trader

- IT @ max 45%
- NIC max @ 10.25%
- POAs
  - 31 January in tax year
  - 31 July after tax year
- Balance 31 January after tax year
- CGT on disposal of chargeable assets
- BPR for IHT if transfer whole business

Company

- CT @ 19% (main rate increasing to 25% from FY23)
- Trading profit benefits from CAs super-deduction and R&D additional relief
- Extracted profit taxable at IT rates
- NIC for:
  - Employee: max @13.25%
  - Employer: max @ 15.05%
- Operate PAYE
- CT paid 9m and one day after AP end
- Gains:
  - CT on disposal of chargeable assets
  - Proceeds extracted at IT rates
- BPR for IHT on any number of unquoted trading company shares

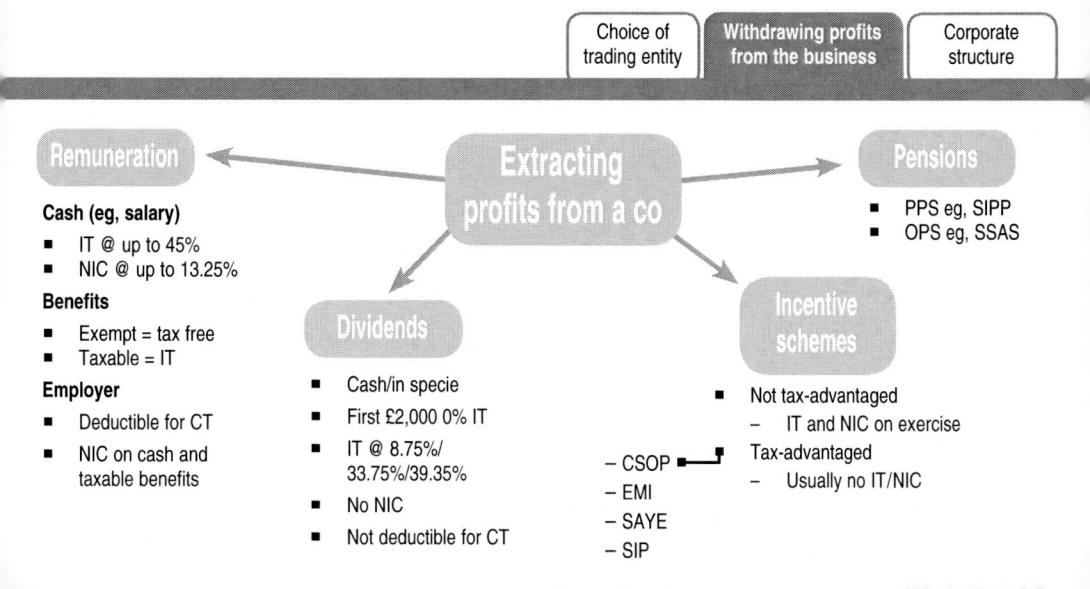

Remuneration

Cash (eg, salary)

- IT @ up to 45%
- NIC @ up to 13.25%

Benefits

- Exempt = tax free
- Taxable = IT

Employer

- Deductible for CT
- NIC on cash and taxable benefits

Extracting profits from a co

Pensions

- PPS eg, SIPP
- OPS eg, SSAS

Dividends

- Cash/in specie
- First £2,000 0% IT
- IT @ 8.75%/ 33.75%/39.35%
- No NIC
- Not deductible for CT

Incentive schemes

- Not tax-advantaged
  - IT and NIC on exercise
- Tax-advantaged
  - Usually no IT/NIC

- CSOP
- EMI
- SAYE
- SIP

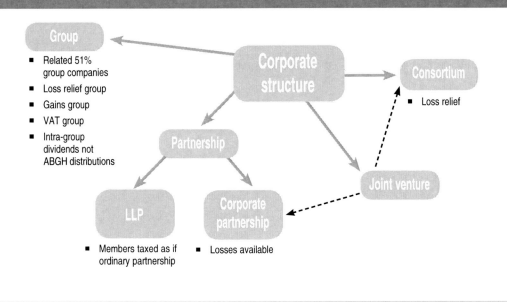

20: Property businesses

You must be able to advise on the varying tax implications of different types of property business.

Topic List

Property businesses

Residential property letting

Residential property development

Commercial property

Property businesses

Choice of business structure

Different types of investment

Residential vs Commercial

'Flipping' vs letting

Company ownership of property

Individual ownership of property

NR companies charged to CT on UK property income

Residential property letting (Buy-to-Let)

	Individual	Company
SDLT	■ Residential property rates plus additional 3% (for second property) and 2% if non-resident	■ Residential property rates plus additional 3% and 2% if non-resident ■ 15% SDLT if single dwelling > £500,000
ATED	■ Does not apply	■ Payable on a dwelling > £500,000
VAT	■ Purchase/sale of new residential – zero rated ■ Purchase/sale existing residential – exempt ■ Most leases – exempt ■ No OTT on residential property	■ As for individual
IT/CT	■ Allowable deduction for domestic items ■ Restriction on finance costs ■ Rent-a-room ■ Accruals basis for receipts over £150k otherwise cash basis	■ Accruals basis ■ Allowable deduction for domestic items ■ Finance costs are NLTR debits ■ Taxed at 19% (potentially up to 25% from FY23)

	Individual	**Company**
	▪ Taxed at 20%/40% and 45%	▪ Extracted profits subject to income tax (salary/dividend)
Losses	▪ Pool in a tax year ▪ Carry forward against property income	▪ Pool in a tax year ▪ Relieve property losses against total income in the year, then carry forward against total income ▪ NTLR deficits on finance cost can be relieved (see earlier)
Gains	▪ CGT at 18%/28 ─────●	▪ CT at 19%
IHT	▪ Properties in death estate (no RNRB) ▪ No BPR on death ─────●	▪ Shares in death estate ▪ No BPR (investment business)

Except FHLs ●

Residential property development ('flipping' properties)

Individuals: differences from letting

- No restriction on finance costs
- PRR may be available if it has been used by the individual
- BPR may be available for construction business
- SDLT additional 3% can be avoided in certain limited situations

Company: preferred route?

- No interest relief restriction
- Profits and gains at 19%
- Possible BPR on shares

Commercial property

	Individual	Company
SDLT	■ Non-residential property rates	■ As for individual
VAT	■ Construction/sale of new non-residential standard rated ■ Improving existing commercial – standard rated ■ Sale of older building – exempt ■ Leases – exempt ■ OTT available	■ As for individual
IT/CT	■ Taxed at 20%/40% and 45%	■ Taxed at 19% ■ Extracted profits subject to income tax (salary/dividend)

	Individual	Company
Losses	▪ Pool in a tax year ▪ Carry forward against property income	▪ Pool in a tax year ▪ Relieve property losses against total income in the year, then carry forward against total income ▪ NLTR deficits on finance cost can be relieved (see earlier)
Gains	▪ CGT at 10%/20%	▪ CT at 19%
IHT	▪ Properties in death estate (no RNRB) ▪ Possible BPR on death (property development)	▪ Shares in death estate ▪ Possible BPR on death (property development)

21: Transformation of owner-managed businesses

Topic List

Incorporation

Disincorporation

Bankruptcy

You must be able to advise on and calculate the tax liabilities arising from the incorporation of an unincorporated business and the disincorporation of a company.

You must also be able to advise on and calculate the tax liabilities arising from the bankruptcy of an individual.

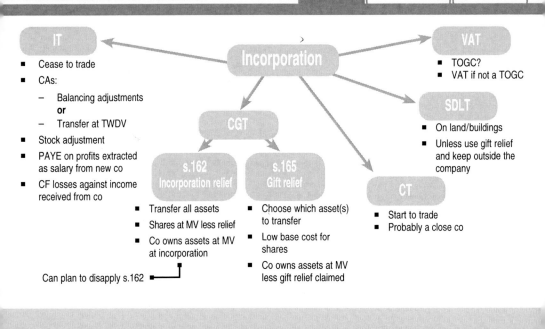

Incorporation

IT
- Cease to trade
- CAs:
  - Balancing adjustments
    or
  - Transfer at TWDV
- Stock adjustment
- PAYE on profits extracted as salary from new co
- CF losses against income received from co

VAT
- TOGC?
- VAT if not a TOGC

SDLT
- On land/buildings
- Unless use gift relief and keep outside the company

CGT

s.162 Incorporation relief
- Transfer all assets
- Shares at MV less relief
- Co owns assets at MV at incorporation

Can plan to disapply s.162

s.165 Gift relief
- Choose which asset(s) to transfer
- Low base cost for shares
- Co owns assets at MV less gift relief claimed

CT
- Start to trade
- Probably a close co

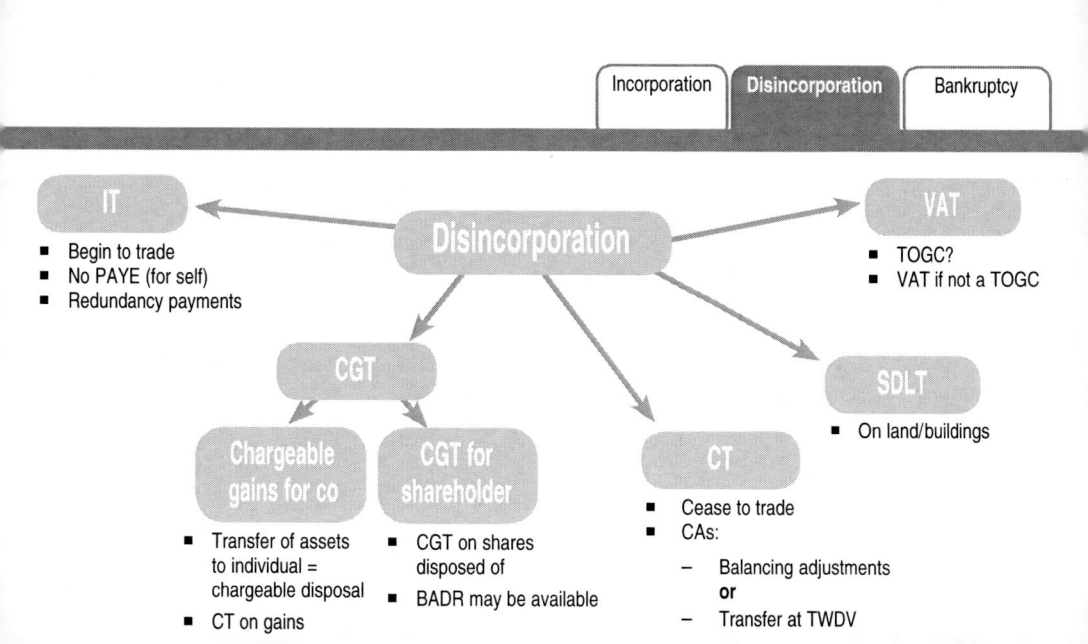

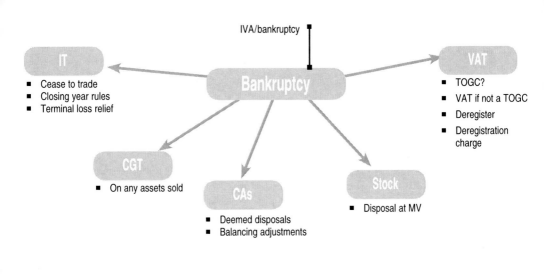

22: Corporate reorganisations

Topic List

Disposing of a corporate business

Sale of shares

Sale of trade and assets

Transfer of a trade within a 75% group

Hive downs

You must be able to advise on, and calculate the tax liabilities arising from, the disposal of a corporate business, the transfer of a trade within a group and the hive down of a trade.

You must also be able to advise on and explain the tax implications of a management buy out.

Sale of shares vs sale of assets

Sale of shares	Sale of assets
Shareholder selling shares	**Company selling assets**
Capital gain/loss	Capital gain/loss on disposals
B/f capital losses reduce gain	IFA disposals = taxable credits/allowable debits
Reduce gain by pre-sale dividend	<ul><li>Balancing adjustments for CAs</li><li>Unless elect to transfer at TWDV</li></ul>
Defer gain if share for share (paper for paper)	Rollover relief may be available
	<ul><li>If sells trade, will cease to trade</li><li>AP ends</li><li>Trading losses lost</li></ul>
SD at 0.5% by purchaser of shares	SDLT at up to 5% by purchaser of land and buildings (assuming non-residential)
Exempt share sale for VAT	<ul><li>VAT payable unless TOGC</li><li>Property may still be subject to VAT</li><li>Usage adjustment for CGS assets</li></ul>

Sale of shares vs sale of assets

Sale of shares	Sale of assets
Corporate shareholders	**Corporate shareholders of company**
SSE may apply to gain	■ Extract after-tax proceeds as dividend ■ Usually exempt ■ May be an ABGH distribution
Group implications: ■ Reduction in related 51% group companies ■ Loss of group relief ■ Degrouping charge for gains	
Individual shareholders	**Individual shareholders of company**
Reliefs for gains: ■ EIS/SEIS	■ Take funds as income (dividend) or capital (if part of liquidation)

Advantages of share deal	Disadvantages of share deal
Vendor	**Vendor**
- No double tax charge – only tax gain on shares	- Degrouping charge
- SSE available	**Purchaser**
- AP does not end	- Assets acquired at TWDV
- No CA balancing adjustments	- Contingent liabilities pass to co
Purchaser	
- Losses of target company available	
- Stamp duty at 0.5%	
- Legally straightforward as contracts pass with co	

Advantages of asset deal

Vendor
- Rollover relief may be available

Purchaser
- MV usually > TWDV
- May create tax-deductible goodwill
- Roll gains over into new assets
- Uplift to MV for assets
- Legal liabilities remain with vendor

Disadvantages of asset deal

Vendor
- CA balancing charge may arise
- Possible further gain on liquidation

Purchaser
- Losses remain with vendor
- SDLT @ up to 5% on land and buildings (assuming non-residential)
- Irrecoverable VAT may arise
- Must transfer contracts so legally = more complex

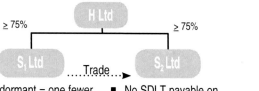

H Ltd

≥ 75% ≥ 75%

S₁ Ltd ·····Trade····▶ **S₂ Ltd**

- SDLT payable if S₂ Ltd sold < three years

- If becomes dormant = one fewer related 51% group company
- Assets transfer at nil gain/nil loss
- Unrelieved capital losses do not pass to S₂
- Trading losses pass to S₂
- Assets transfer at TWDV so no CA balancing adjustments

- No SDLT payable on land/buildings received
- Degrouping charge if company sold < six years of transfer
- Trading losses received

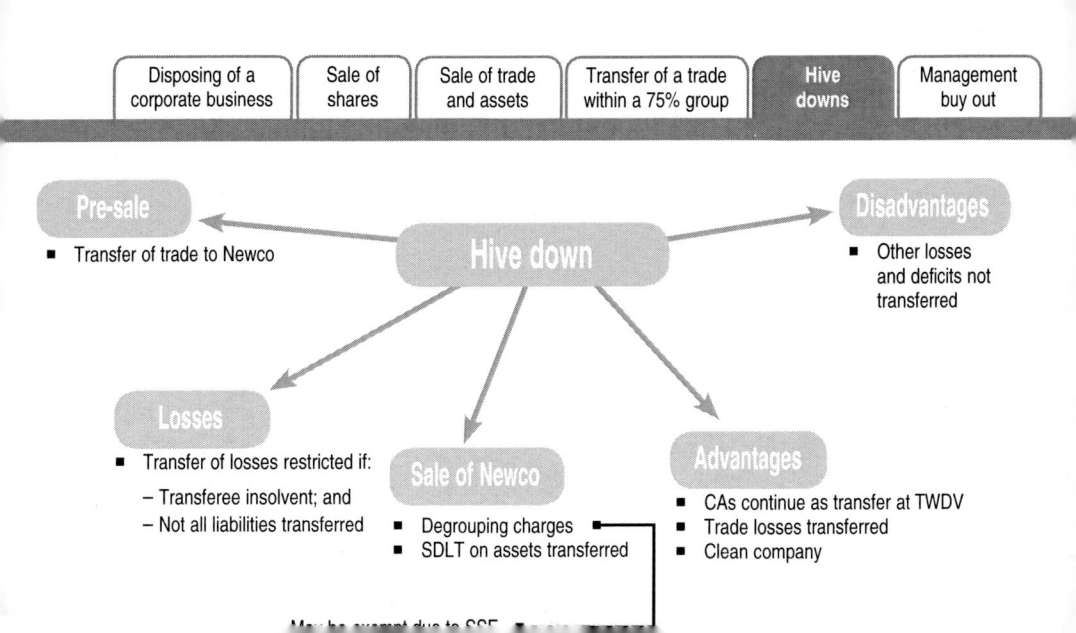

Hive down

Pre-sale
- Transfer of trade to Newco

Disadvantages
- Other losses and deficits not transferred

Losses
- Transfer of losses restricted if:
  - Transferee insolvent; and
  - Not all liabilities transferred

Sale of Newco
- Degrouping charges
- SDLT on assets transferred

Advantages
- CAs continue as transfer at TWDV
- Trade losses transferred
- Clean company

May be exempt due to SSE

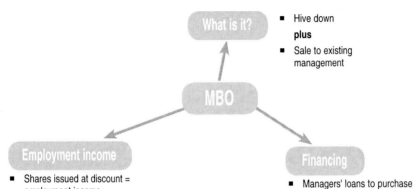

What is it?

- Hive down
  plus
- Sale to existing management

MBO

Employment income

- Shares issued at discount = employment income
- Shares partly paid up = employee beneficial loan

Financing

- Managers' loans to purchase shares = deductible qualifying interest
- Company – loan relationship rules